# INDIANS
# *of North America*

## Methods and Sources
## for Library Research

*Marilyn L. Haas*

Library Professional Publications
1983

© 1983 Marilyn L. Haas. All rights reserved.
First published 1983 as a Library Professional Publication,
an imprint of the Shoe String Press, Inc.
Hamden, Connecticut 06514

Printed in the United States of America

The paper in this book meets the guidelines for permanence
and durability of the Committee on Production Guidelines
for Book Longevity of the Council on Library Resources.

Library of Congress Cataloging in Publication Data

Haas, Marilyn L.
    Indians of North America.

    Includes index.
    1. Indians of North America — Bibliography.
2. Indians of North America — Library resources — United
States.   3. Reference books — Indians of North America.
4. Indians of North America — Research — Methodology.
I. Title.
Z1209.H22   1983 [E77]     016.970004'97     83–14007
ISBN  0-208-01980-4

# INDIANS
## *of North America*

# Contents

# Foreword

As Americans become increasingly aware of the important contributions of cultural minorities in all areas of our national life, researchers and the librarians who assist them discover that there are many problems of access to pertinent materials. Authors and editors are striving to make significant revisions in textbooks and to promote the publication of literature that reverses the stereotypical images of the past. Minority people themselves as well as members of the majority cultures wish to have revealed more clearly the beauty and values of the minority cultures as they have been and continue to be woven into the social fabric of America. These efforts have already borne fruit, and much fuller use could be made of the excellent materials that are already available, but sometimes difficult to obtain for use. Bibliographic guides have been compiled for black, Hispanic, and more recently, Asian materials; in the area of American Indian materials, however, many of the materials are not easily located through the usual sources.

In this work, Marilyn Haas has produced a reference tool which provides not only a significant compilation of resources of North American Indians, but the means of access to them. Her careful and detailed outlining of step-by-step procedures, based on her experience as a reference librarian, is a unique contribution in this field. Nowhere else does the user find this kind of helpful guidance to the utilization of material.

Designed to be self-instructional, this reference work will be especially helpful to those who are not very familiar with library research strategies. Both secondary school and college students will find the pragmatic discussion on library methodology useful and the extensive guides to material invaluable. Others, such as scholars who will find the key to more obscure sources described here, and librarians who will appreciate the thoroughness of Ms. Haas's citations, can use the tool to trace esoteric items as well as the more commonplace ones.

The contents and organization of the work will be particularly helpful to tribal persons who are seeking information, and it should be used as a first step in helping them to locate desired material. The growing need for information among Indian people about themselves and their heritage as they continue to develop their tenets for self-determination, has resulted in a growing demand for access to resources. This reference tool provides a basic path to acquisition, as it identifies possible sources. In the near future on-line searching through the data bases described here will supply the next step, and interlibrary loan networks—of which Indian reservation and near reservation libraries will, it is to be hoped, be a part—will complete the process by getting information into the hands of people who need it.

While a number of titles contained in this reference tool are well known to frequent library users, others, like the book catalogs of individual libraries, are not. Their inclusion gives helpful direction toward a whole new array of sources. Also useful are the discussions and titles given in the chapter on archives and government sources. These chapters together with the careful delineation of other indexes, abstracts and on-line data bases combine to give the user a complete overview to resources on the Indian people of the North American continent.

The value of this work is twofold: one, in introducing users to the most appropriate methodology for searching the subject; and two, in its comprehensive listing of the sources of Indian material. The author has made a significant contribution to the field of librarianship by providing a tool that is both pragmatic in approach and extensive in coverage. Students, teachers, scholars, librarians, and tribal people are all indebted to Ms. Haas for a work that is long overdue.

DR. LOTSEE PATTERSON SMITH
*Member of the Comanche Tribe*
*Associate Professor, Texas Women's University*
*President, American Indian Library Association*

# Preface

This is a guide to library research on North American Indians (i.e., Indians living in the geographic area that is now the United States and Canada). It is meant to help college students writing papers, Indians studying their tribal history, anthropologists and archaeologists, historians and hobbyists, teachers of Indian children, lawyers seeking background information — and the librarians who help them all — to find written information on North American Indians.

The book is in three parts. The first part covers library methodology and reference works. Methodology includes subject headings, classification systems and call numbers; reference works covers indexes, abstracts, on-line data bases, book catalogs, encyclopedias, directories, and the like, including tools for using government documents and archives.

The second part is an annotated bibliography of books on topics useful in Indian study: agriculture, alcohol, archaeology, art, and so on through the alphabet. Books in this second part include standard monographs or subject bibliographies, or both, and if there are journals appropriate to that particular topic, they are also listed. The "standard" monographs listed are just that. Their choice is not meant to imply that they are necessarily the best books on the subject — simply that they are accepted, useful works which can serve as a first step into a topic.

Subject headings for each category in this second part are also given since, with the proper subject heading, more books on a topic can be found. (The concept of subject headings is an essential and often overlooked part of library methodology. Their use is emphasized throughout this book.)

The third part of the book is an unannotated list of books on individual tribes.

The works listed in the first and second sections of the book are limited to those which cover many North American Indian groups (as opposed to those which cover single tribes or narrow geographic areas). They are also, with some few exceptions, limited to those published since 1970 and to those in the English language.

In addition to aiding librarians, I hope this book can also serve as a self-teaching manual for those unfamiliar with library practice. For this reason, nothing is taken for granted. The purpose served by each kind of reference tool is explained briefly and library terms are defined as they appear.

# To the Beginning Researcher

This book speaks to the intellectual part of library research. You can use it effectively only after you already know your way around a library.

If you are new to a particular library, walk around it to get an idea of its physical layout. Find out where the restrooms are, the clocks, the pencil sharpeners, the telephone, the typing room, the nearest snack bar. If you are a college student, don't wait until the deadline for your paper is almost upon you to do this. Large libraries can look alarmingly like a maze on your first visit.

Find out where the copy machines are. For a little change (bring some with you) you can make copies of pages in books that cannot be checked out — such as encyclopedias — or copies of pages that are especially tedious to make notes from — columns of statistics, for example.

Look up a book in the catalog that you want to read just for fun: a novel, or a book on sports, or poetry, or science fiction, or even on Indians. Go and get it in the stacks (the floors where the books are shelved). Check the locations of the elevators and the stairs. Do this, and later when you really need to find a book you will know your way around.

Locate the current and the bound magazines and newspapers. "Current" means recent, usually this year. "Bound" refers to older magazines in which all of the issues for one year (generally) are bound together into one volume which then looks like a book. (Magazines in a library are usually called journals or periodicals because they come out periodically.)

Find out where the microforms are. Noncurrent journals and newspapers, especially newspapers, may not be bound. They may exist in the library only on some kind of microform, most likely microfilm, which looks like ordinary movie film. (Some libraries have a machine called a reader-printer so that you can make a paper copy of the microfilm.) If the library has anything on microfilm, it is apt to be the *New York Times*. Ask to see the *New York Times* for the day on which you were born, or for any other date you might want to read about. (For example, the events at Wounded Knee, South Dakota, of 30 and 31 December 1890 and again in March, April, and May of 1973 were both reported in the *New York Times*.)

If you are in a large library system, make sure you are in the right library. Large libraries have specialized units or branches. Art, music, law, medicine, are common examples. If your particular interest lies in one of those fields, you probably ought to be in one of those libraries.

If the library offers regular orientation tours, take one. While you are following the guide, think how what he or she is telling you will help with your particular research interest.

If a computerized bibliographic search demonstration is offered, go. Computer demonstrations are fun.

Ask the right people for help. (Don't ask the people beside you at the card catalog. They may be as confused as you are.) For questions on how to write papers, how to find books and articles on specific topics, talk to the people at the reference or information desk. For questions on checking out books, in fact, *to* check out books, go to the circulation desk. (These two desks serve quite different functions.)

A library is a treasure house of information. Learn how to use it and you will have a key to the treasure and a skill that will give you pleasure all of your life.

To write this book I have drawn on my experience at the reference desk of a university library and also on my article "A Basic Guide to Reference Sources for the Study of the North American Indian," *Reference Services Review* 7, no. 1 (July/September 1979): 15–35, which started out in 1976 as "The North American Indian, Information Sources in Lockwood Library," a six-page handout for students at the State University of New York at Buffalo.

MARILYN L. HAAS

# Part 1

# *Library Methodology and Reference Works*

# 1

# Subject Headings, Classification Systems and Call Numbers

Most library users have the correct idea that the card catalog is the index to the holdings of a library, that there are author, title, and subject cards for every book in the library, and that these cards are arranged alphabetically.

In other words, if the author or title of a book is known, the book can be looked up in the author-title part of a catalog and assuming the author's name is spelled right, or the title is correct, one can find the book.

## SUBJECT HEADINGS

When no author or title is known, books on a subject are found by using the subject part of a catalog. American library catalogs tend to come in two styles: dictionary and divided. "Dictionary" means that authors, titles, and subjects are all together in one alphabetical arrangement, and "divided" means that author and title are in one alphabetical file and subjects in another. Either way, the subjects are arranged by standard subject headings (the words one looks under to find information on the subject of interest). As many library users have trouble phrasing their topic the way a library card catalog does, especially in regard to American Indian material, here are some guidelines to subject headings as they apply when doing research in this field.

These are broad guidelines. Subject headings are subject to local variations and they do change (slowly) through time. There is enough consistency to them, however, so that a knowledge of the pattern is helpful.

Most American libraries beyond the high-school level use the subject heading list published by the Library of Congress, *Library of Congress Subject Headings*, 9th ed. 2 vols. (Washington, D.C.; 1980). These big red books are always kept by the card catalog. In

3

this list, many books concerning the North American Indian are listed under a phrase beginning "Indians of North America" which is then modified by the particular topic. These topics can be quite narrow ("Indians of North America—Water rights"; "Indians of North America—Alcohol use") or they can be broad ("Indians of North America—Education"; "Indians of North America—Government relations"; "Indians of North America—Social life and customs"; "Indians of North America—Antiquities [the subject heading for many books about New World archaeology]).

The headings may also be subdivided geographically ("Indians of North America—California"; "Indians of North America—Canada"; "Indians of North America—the West").

These two kinds of headings may also be combined ("Indians of North America—California—Government relations"; "Indians of North America—New Mexico—Antiquities").

The point is, then, if you are looking in the *subject* card catalog under "American Indians" or "Amerinds" or "Native American," you are *not* going to find books on Indians. You must phrase your topic the way the Library of Congress subject heading book does.

There are of course, more specific headings for more specific topics. Religious ceremonies, battles, reservations, may also be subject headings ("Sun dance"; "Sullivan's Indian Campaign, 1779"; "Pine Ridge Indian Reservation, South Dakota").

Individual tribal names are also used as appropriate ("Cherokee Indians," "Navajo Indians," "Osage Indians"). The most specific subject heading possible is chosen for a book. If the book is on one tribe only, it will have that tribe's name as a subject heading. It will not *also* be under "Indians of North America". If the tribe has several different names, or one name has several different spellings, the subject part of the card catalog will use only one of these names. There may, *or there may not*, be cross-references referring from the name not used to the name used. The names actually used are listed in *Subject Headings*. Example: there is nothing in the card catalog under "Ojibwa." The subject heading book is consulted. Here it says "Ojibwa Indians *see* Chippewa Indians." This means that while there may be *titles* starting with the word "Ojibwa" in the catalog, by subject, all books dealing with this tribe will be filed under the word "Chippewa." ("Sioux Indians *see* Dakota Indians"; "Wabanaki Indians *see* Abnaki Indians"; "Absahrokee (or Absaroka, or Apsaroke) Indians *see* Crow Indians" are other applications of this rule.) (A list of Indian tribes of North America is on pp. 885–887 of *Subject Headings*, v. 1.)*

People's names may also be subject headings. (Individuals without a surname are entered under their name followed by an identifying phrase — "Joseph, Nez Perce Chief"; "Crashing Thunder, Winnebago Indian"; "Black Elk, Oglala Indian," and so on.)

The subject headings may also be modified by the *form* of the book. "Dictionary," "bibliography," are typical form modifications. Thus, if a book is a language dictionary, the subject heading could be, for example, "Mohawk language — Dictionary." If it is a bibliography, the heading could be "Indians of North America — Bibliogaphy," or if on one tribe, "Hopi Indians — Bibliography," and so on.

Despite these guidelines it is sometimes hard to phrase a topic in library catalog terms. One easy way to find more books on a subject you are interested in is to check the subject headings assigned to a book that you already know is on target. Look up the book in the card catalog (by author) and check the subject headings printed at the bottom of the card. Then look up these exact subject headings in the subject part of the catalog. If you have the book in hand, a still easier way to do this (for many American books printed in recent years) is to look at the "Cataloging in Publication" data on the back of the title page. Here, in what is almost a replica of a Library of Congress card, you can see what subject headings have been assigned to this particular book and therefore are appropriate to your search.

Once the card for a pertinent book is found in the card catalog, the call number in the upper left hand corner of the card tells where the book is shelved in the library. The call numbers are derived from the classification systems used.

Call numbers, of course, like subject headings are subject to local variation and they too change through time. However, again like subject headings, there is a rational structure behind them and therefore behind the numbers on the spine of a book, and a little knowledge about this structure is useful.

(Copies of catalog cards illustrating subject headings and call numbers follow.)

---

*The name of the Navajo tribe is spelled with the "j" in most citations, but the Library of Congress uses the "h" spelling. The "j" is used throughout this book except in the Bibliography by Tribe heading.

## SAMPLE LIBRARY OF CONGRESS CARDS

*Subject heading*

**Hodge, William H.,** 1932–
   The first Americans: then and now / William H. Hodge. – New York: Holt, Rinehart, and Winston, c1981.
xx, 551 p.:ill.; 25 cm.
Includes bibliographical references and index.
ISBN 0-03-056721-1

*Subject heading with geographic modification*

1. Indians of North America. I. Title
E77.H695        970.004'97 – dc19
Library of Congress

*Indicates 19th edition of Dewey was used*

**Russell, Howard S.**
   Indian New England before the Mayflower/Howard S. Russell. – Hanover, N.H.: University Press of New England, 1980.
xi, 284 p.: ill.; 24 cm.
Bibliography: p. 237–270.
Includes index.
ISBN 0-87451-162-3: $17.50

*Library of Congress call number*

1. Indians of North America – New England – History.     I. Title.
E78.N5R87        974'.00497 – dc19
Library of Congress  80

*Dewey Decimal number (One of these numbers would be in the upper left-hand corner depending on which system is used in the library.)*

**Murdock, George Peter,** 1897.
   Ethnographic bibliography of North America/George Peter Murdock and Timothy J. O'Leary, with the assistance of John Beierle . . . [et al.]. – 4th ed. – New Haven: Human Relations Area Files Press, 1975.
5 v.: maps: 29 cm. – (Behavior science bibliographies)
CONTENTS: v. 1. General North America. – v. 2 Arctic and subarctic. – v. 3. Far West and Pacific coast. – v. 4. Eastern United States. – v. 5. Plains and Southwest.
ISBN 0–87536-205-2 (v. 1)

*Subject heading with form modification*

1. Indians of North America – Bibliography. I. O'Leary, Timothy J., joint author.   II. Title.   III. Series.
Z1209.2.N67M87    1975   016.97'0004'97
[E77]
Library of Congress

*Subject heading modified both geographically and by the form of the book.*

**Bramstedt, Wayne G.**
   A bibliography of North American Indians in the Los Angeles metropolitan area, the urban Indian capital/Wayne G. Bramstedt – Monticello, Ill.: Vance Bibliographies, 1979.
14 p.; 28 cm. – (Public administration series: Bibliography; P. 233)
Cover title.
$1.50

1. Indians of North America – California – Los Angeles metropolitan area – Bibliography. 2. Indians of North America – Urban residence – Bibliography.
I. Title.   II. Series.
Z1209.2.U52C223    016.30145'19'7079494
[E78–C15]
Library of Congress  79

**Haley, James L.**
    Apaches, a history and culture portrait/James L.
Haley. — 1st ed. — Garden City, N.Y.: Doubleday, 1981.
xxi, 453 p. [32] leaves of plates: ill.; 24 cm.
Bibliography: p. [416]–437.
Includes index.
ISBN 0–385–12147–4: $17.95

*There may be one subject heading*

1. Apache Indians — History.   I. Title.
E99.A6H24        970.004'97 — dc19

Library of Congress    80

OR

**Schwartz, Douglas Wright, 1929–**
    Archaeology of the Grand Canyon: Unkar Delta/Douglas
W. Schwartz, Richard C. Chapman, Jane Kepp. — 1st ed. —
Santa Fe, NM: School of American Research Press, c1980.
xvi, 405 p.: ill.; 23 cm. — (Grand Canyon archaeological series; v.2)
Bibliography: p. 401–405.
ISBN 0–933452–04–7: $8.95

*there may be up to seven subject headings.*

1. Indians of North America — Arizona — Unkar Creek — Delta — An-
tiquities. 2. Unkar Creek, Ariz. — Delta Antiquities. 3. Arizona — An-
tiquities. 4. Excavations (Archaeology) — Arizona — Unkar Creek —
Delta. 5. Cohonina culture. 6. Pueblo Indians — Antiquities. 7. Grand
Canyon — Antiquities. I. Chapman, Richard C., joint author. II. Kepp,
Jane, joint author. III. Title. IV. Series.
E78.A7G69        vol. 2        979.1'32s — dc19

*(There would be twelve cards for this book: one for each of these "tracings," and one for the main author.)*

Library of Congress

## CLASSIFICATION SYSTEMS AND CALL NUMBERS

The purpose of a classification system is to put like subjects together.* A book classification system accordingly divides all knowledge into major classes and assigns numbers, or a combination of letters and numbers, to each class. The resulting classification system is then used again and again. Libraries in North America, indeed throughout the world, use primarily two systems of classification, the Dewey Decimal and the Library of Congress. The Dewey Decimal divides all knowledge into nine classes numbered 100 to 900. Materials too general for a specific group — encyclopedias, etc. — are put in a tenth class, 000, which precedes the others. (Bibliographies are also put into this class.) The Library of Congress divides all knowledge into twenty-one classes and assigns a combination of letters and numbers to its classes.

In the Dewey system, books on American Indians generally have a number which starts 970 (the class number for general

---

*This is a bare-bones summary of library classification systems. The interested reader is referred to Jean Key Gates, *Guide to the Use of Books and Libraries*, 3d ed. (New York: McGraw-Hill, 1974) 41–58 for a clear discussion of the Dewey and Library of Congress systems.

history of North America). Large libraries using the 19th edition of Dewey may modify this number to 970.00497. Libraries using earlier editions of Dewey use 970.1 or 970.5, or thereabouts, depending on the size of the library, which edition of Dewey the cataloger was using, and the exact subject covered.

The 970 class, of course, is not the only place where Indian books are classified. Indian bibliographies are in the 016.97 class; books on religion and mythology in the 299.7 class; legal problems, 342; legends, 398; language, 497–498; art, 709.1; literature, 810–811; 897–898; and so on. (This is not an exhaustive list.)

In the Library of Congress classification system, which this book will focus on since it is used by most large libraries, the range E51–E99 includes most of the books on North American Indians. Some of the other places in the Library of Congress schedule which may logically have Indian books are GN, anthropology; F, United States local history and Canada; KF, legal material; PM, Indian languages; PN, literary history and collections; PS, American literature; R, medicine; and Z, bibliography.

The above numbers or letter-number combinations are the "class" numbers. They make up the top line of a call number and put together all books on the same subject. (The second line of a call number is the "book" or "author" number. It distinguishes one book on the same subject from another.)

These class numbers are useful for browsing, and browsing is a good way to get a feel for what a library has on a subject. Browsing should never, however, take the place of checking the card catalog in serious research since the very book needed may be checked out, or the scattering effect of library classification systems may have put the book into a class not even considered.

An abbreviated outline of the E51–E99 range and of the other Library of Congress classes not in this range which have Indian material follows.

## LIBRARY OF CONGRESS CLASSES THAT HAVE BOOKS ON NORTH AMERICAN INDIANS

| | |
|---|---|
| E51–E61 | Pre-Columbian America. The Indians. |
| E71 | North America (north of Mexico). |
| E73–E74 | Mound Builders. |
| | *Indians of North America* |
| E75 | Periodicals.  Societies.  Collections. |

| | |
|---|---|
| E76 | Congresses. Dictionaries. Directories. Guides to tribes. Study and teaching. Research. Historiography. |
| E77 | General Works. |
| E78 | Works by state, province, or region, A–Z. (For example, books on Indians of Arizona would have the call number E78.A7; books on Iowa Indians, E78.I6; Canada, (general) E78.C2; British Columbia, E78.B9; Northwest coast of North America, E78.N78.) |
| E81–E83 | Indian Wars. |
| E85–E87 | Captivities. |
| E89 | Biography (Collective). |
| E90 | Biography (Individual). |
| E91 | Government relations (general works). |
| E92 | Government relations (Canada). |
| E93 | Government relations (United States). |
| E94 | Laws (Collections). } See also the K classes. |
| E95 | Treaties (Collections). |
| E97 | Education. |
| E98 | Other topics, A–Z, for example, art, E98.A7; children, E98.C5; games, E98.G2; religion, mythology, E98.R3; social life and customs, E98.S7; women, E98.W8. |
| E99 | Tribes, A–Z (Examples: Arapaho, E99.A7; Fox, E99.F7; Kwakiutl, E99.K9; Zuni, E99.Z9.) |
| F1–F975 | The United States local history class. Books on Indians of a specific locality may have an F classification. |
| F697–F698 | Indian Territory history. |
| F1001–F1140 | British America. Canada. Books on Canadian Indians particularly by the early explorers may have a F classification. |
| GN | The anthropology class. Indian books are in this class if they are part of an anthropology series or if the treatment is primarily anthropological. |
| HD231–HD234 | Indian lands. (Older books on land transfers, leases, etc., may be.here. The K and E classes are now more frequently used.) |

| | |
|---|---|
| KE* | The law of Canada class. |
| KE318.N3 | Indian law students. |
| KE378.N3 | Legal aid. |
| KE7701–KE7710 | Native people. |
| KE7715 | Land laws. Reserves and settlements. |
| KE7718 | Claims. |
| KE7722 | Other topics, A–Z. (For example, education KE7722.E3; hunting and fishing rights, KE7722.H8.) |
| KE7735 | Indigenous legal system – general works. |
| KE7739 | Indigenous legal systems – special topics. |
| KE7742 | Indigenous legal systems – administration. |
| KE7749 | Indigenous legal systems – particular groups or topics, A–Z. |
| KE1044 | Native people – Ontario. |
| KE1060 | Native people – Quebec. |
| | |
| KF* | The law of the United States class. |
| KF5660–KF5662 | Indian lands. |
| KF8201–KF8228 | Indian legal matters. (If the book is on Indian laws of a particular state the KF will be followed by a third letter – KFC, California; KFN, New York.) |
| | |
| L | The education class. |
| | |
| LC2629 | Education of Indians in Canada. (Most books on education are in the E97 class.) |
| | |
| M | The music class. |
| M1669 | Indian vocal music. |
| | |
| ML3557 | Writing on North American Indian music. (E59.M9 or E98.M9 may also have books on Indian music.) |
| | |
| N | The art class. |
| N8217.I5 | Indians in art. (Used for Indians as subject matter – generally Indian art books are in E59.A7 or E98.A7.) |

---

*The K classes were not fully developed until the 1960s, consequently many law libraries do not use the Library of Congress system, or use it only for books published since that time.

| | |
|---|---|
| PE1127.I5 | Indians of North America — juvenile literature (i.e., readers.) |
| PM | The American Indian language class. |
| PM101–PM149 | Indian languages, texts in Indian languages. |
| PM155–PM198 | Indian literature, poetry and its history and criticism; translations into English or other languages. |
| PM201–PM2711 | Indian languages. (Dictionaries, grammars, etc.) |
| PN | The class for literary history and collections. |
| PN1995.9.I48 | American Indians in motion pictures. |
| PN4883 | Indian newspapers. |
| PN6120.I6 | Indians of North America — Drama. |
| PS | The American literature class. |
| PS153.I52 | History and criticism of the fiction of Indian authors. |
| PS173.I6 | Indians in literature — criticism. |
| PS508.I5 | American Indian author collections. |
| PS591.I55 | American Indian poetry. |
| R | The medicine class. |
| RA448.5.I5 | Public health aspects concerning Indians. |
| RA801 | Indians of North America — Health and Hygiene. |
| RA981.A35 | Indian hospitals. |
| RC451.5.I5 | Indian mental health. |
| Z | The bibliography class. |
| Z1208 | American archaeology bibliography. |
| Z1209–Z1210 | American Indian bibliography. |
| Z1229.I3 | American Indian authors bibliography. |
| Z7116–Z7119 | American Indian language bibliography. |

# 2

# Indexes

The preceding chapter told how to find books that a library owns. Much of the information in a library, however, is not in books, but is in magazines (usually called journals, or periodicals, in library jargon). Unlike books, journals can have current information. (The information in a book is at least a year old before it reaches a library.) Journal articles are shorter than books—an advantage when in-depth information is not necessary. The articles can discuss narrower subjects, those that don't require book-length treatment, and they are furthermore the place where the current news and the new ideas and theories of a discipline first appear.

Library card catalogs do not ordinarily have subject cards for journal articles,* so information in them must be found by using the indexing and abstracting services. (An index tells where an article is, that is, what journal it is in. An abstract tells where it is and gives a short summary of it as well. The summary may have enough information in itself, and if it does not, it at least gives enough information so that you can decide whether or not to follow through and read the entire article.)

It is not possible to draw a hard line between indexing and abstracting services. Some services with "index" in their name also have a substantial number of abstracts (*Religion Index One: Periodicals*), and some services with "abstract" in their title actually only index many of the articles they include (*Women Studies Abstracts*). For convenience, this section first describes those publications which call themselves indexes followed by those which call themselves abstracts. Either kind of service will usually have an author and subject approach. (Title listings are uncommon and generally used only for

---

*Exceptions are some of the great specialized research libraries which will be discussed in the chapter on book catalogs.

literary works.) Many articles, of course, do not have a named author so the subject approach is paramount.

## INDEXES

The most commonly available and currently published indexes are listed here first. The "ceased-publication" and more specialized indexes follow.

Leading off this section are the steady workhorses of a library's reference collection—the indexes published by the H. W. Wilson Company. The *Readers' Guide to Periodical Literature*[1] is the key to current information in general magazines. *Readers' Guide* indexes a wide spectrum of mainstream* magazines which people read for news and for entertainment. In 1981, for example, there were references to articles on Indian land tenure problems in Canada (from *Macleans*);† and on the same subject in Maine (from *Newsweek*); and, still on land tenure, but in Massachusetts, (from *People*). There were also citations to articles on the Native American and energy resources and on Indian artists (both from the Roman Catholic *America*). There were references to an article on "evangelical" Indians in *Christianity Today*, (a conservative Protestant magazine); on contemporary problems "Navajo mineral swindle . . . " in *USA Today*; and on Indian business (*Nation's Business*). The picture and hobby magazines are also covered in *Readers' Guide* with citations to articles on Indian agriculture (*National Geographic*); Alaska natives (*Smithsonian*); Indian digging tools (*Hobbies*); beadwork (*Antiques Journal*); and on and on.

*Readers' Guide*, then, does not index the learned journals, but it is the index of choice for current news, and as it stretches back to 1900, it is also the place to check to see how Indian subject matter has been treated over the years. It is also relatively easy to use with generous "see" and "see also" references. A "see" reference instructs you to look under another heading. It is referring from a heading not used to one that is used. Thus: "Indians of North America—Astronomy"

---

*There are several indexes to small press and underground magazines. (*Alternative Press Index*[2] which indexes the leading Indian periodical, *Akwesasne Notes*, is one.) These indexes tend to run about a year behind so they are not the place to go for current information.

†Although *Readers' Guide* does pick up *Macleans*, a more fruitful place to check for current Canadian Indian matters is *Canadian Periodical Index. Index de Periodiques Canadiens.*[3] This is not a Wilson index, but it is similar in format to *Readers' Guide* and it also uses Library of Congress subject headings.

*see* [under] "Astronomy, Indian (American)." A "see also" heading refers you to related subjects you might want to consider: "Indians of North America—Implements" *see also* "Arrowheads." The editors also explain a title if the title is not self-explanatory. (For an article entitled "No acres and no mules," listed under the subject heading "Indians of North America—Land tenure," the editors have supplied the clarifying note "problems dealing with claim lawyers.")

Other Wilson indexes follow generally the same format. Briefer notes on them follow.

See the following pages for sample columns from *Readers' Guide.*

INDIANS of North America—Art—*Continued*
   Turtle for the living arts [Native American Center for the Living Arts, Niagara Falls, N.Y.] W. Trimm. il Conservationist 36:22-6 N/D '81
   Warriors' world: a Cheyenne self-portrait [ledger art; excerpts from People of the sacred mountain] P. J. Powell. il Am Heritage 33:36-43 D '81
      *Exhibitions*
   Art among the Adobes [Santa Fe Festival of the Arts] il Horizon 24:68-9 S '81
      Astronomy
   *See* Astronomy, Indian (American)
      Basket making

Illustrated, illustration illustrator

   Tisket, a tasket, a multi-purpose basket. C. Miles. il Hobbies 85:120-1 F '81
      Child welfare
   Indian child welfare. Child Today 10:24 N/D '81
      Children
      *See also*
   Indians of North America—Child welfare
      Civil rights
   Unfinished charter [constitutional charter of rights in Canada] I. Anderson. il Macleans 94:26-7 N 30 '81
      Claims
      *See also*
   Indians of North America—Land tenure

A "see" heading refers from a heading not used to one that is used.

      Cooking
   *See* Cooking, Indian (American)
      Costume and adornment
   Plains Indians beadwork. B. Evanoff. bibl il Antiques J 36:36-8+ Ag '81
   Puckered or flapped, Indian soles step high in design. C. Miles. il Hobbies 86:108-9 S '81
      Crime
   Cloud of witnesses [murder of K. B. Green by Indians in Arizona] il por Newsweek 99:20 Ja 11 '82

Journal abbreviations are in the front of the book. This one is for *Architectural Record.*

      Dwellings
   From teepee to solar-heated mobile homes: experimental houses for New Mexican Indians. A. Gabor. il Archit Rec 169:36 N '81

## Education

Foster grandparents teach Indian lore and language. V. R. Ashby. il Child Today 10:16-17+ My/Je '81

Indian education: accomplishments of the last decade. R. J. Havighurst. Phi Delta Kappan 62:329-31 Ja '81

Indian Education Act grants. H. Harris. Am Educ 17:28 Jl '81

## Fishing

Big guns for little fishes [police raid against alleged salmon poaching by Quebec's Micmac] D. Thomas. il Macleans 94:18-20 Je 29 '81

Fish story [salmon in Washington state] R. Sokolov. il Natur Hist 90:100-4 Jl '81

## Footwear

*See* Indians of North America—Costume and adornment

## Gifts

Indian peace medals [excerpt from The history of American coinage] Q. D. Bowers. il Hobbies 85:124 F '81

## Government relations

*See also*
Indians of North America—Gifts
Indians of North America—Land tenure
Indians of North America—Wars

Ancient injustice revisited [legal status of New Brunswick Malecite S. Lovelace] D. Folster. il por Macleans 94:13 S 28 '81

Murderer, martyr—or both? The tangled case of the Sioux 'enforcer.' Leonard Peltier. J. Calio. il por People 15:110-11+ Ap 20 '81

Navajo mineral swindle: wheeling and dealing on the reservation [Interior Department vs lawyer N. Littell] M. Miller and others. por USA Today 109:56-60 My '81

### *History*

Indians braved Washington to see the Great Father [excerpt from Diplomats in buckskin] H. J. Viola. il Smithsonian 12:72-80 Ap '81

## History

American Indian through five centuries. J. Cook. il Forbes 128:118+ N 9 '81

Bernal Díaz, meet John Smith. N. M. Scott. il pors Américas 33:32-9 Je/Jl '81

Lion Gardiner and his island. R. Welch. il maps Am Hist Illus 16:40-6 My '81

## Hunting

*See also*
Buffalo hunting

Apache elk [annual hunt sponsored by Apache Indians challenged by Arizona officials] B. Hess. il Field & S 86:52-3+ My '81

Outrage over walrus slaughter [Alaska natives] C. Batin. il Outdoor Life 167:34+ Ap '81

Subsistence hunting in Alaskan parks. J. T. Shively. il Nat Parks 55:18-21 Mr '81

## Implements

*See also*
Tomahawks

Amerind beveled-edged blades. L. Hothem. il Antiques J 36:17-19 Ap '81

Digging tools. C. Miles. il Hobbies 86:108-9 Jl '81

Knives. C. Miles. il Hobbies 86:120-1 Ap '81

Alaska's natives are bringing off the biggest
corporate takeover. M. Parfit. il Smithsonian
12:30-9 Ag '81
Industrial reservation. P. A. Schwab. il Nations Bus 69:54-8 Ag '81
Windfall that hasn't made it yet [Alaska Native Claims Settlement Act] E. Keerdoja. il
Newsweek 99:10 Ja 11 '82

### Land tenure
Growing sense of northern déjà vu [reactivation
of Indian land claims issue as National Energy
Board gives go-ahead to oil pipeline in Mac-
kenzie Valley, Northwest Territories] G. Legge.
il map Macleans 94:40+ My 4 '81
Indian tribe's fight for land beats a warpath
next door to Jackie O. [Wampanoag Indians'
claim to Martha's Vineyard] J. Keller. il
People 16:40-1 S 14 '81
Land, not caviar, for Maine indians [Penobscot
and Passamaquoddy tribes] E. Keerdoja and
D. Shapiro. il Newsweek 98:9 Ag 25 '81
Longhouses in high-rise country? [land claim by
Cree Indian group, the Ballantynes, in Prince-
Albert, Saskatchewan] T. Fennell. il Macleans
94:23-5 F 9 '81
No acres and, no mules [problems dealing with
claims lawyers] P. Shattuck. il Nation 233:
168-70+ S 5 '81
This land is whose land [Canada; with editorial
comment by P. C. Newman] R. MacGregor.
il pors map Macleans 94:3, 49+ Je 1 '81
Windfall that hasn't made it yet [Alaska Na-
tive Claims Settlement Act] E. Keerdoja. il
Newsweek 99:10 Ja 11 '82

Since the title does not
make the subject clear,
an explanatory note
was added in brackets.

### Land utilization
Indian harvest white man style [land tenure
controversy involving use of Sarcee land for
housing development for non-Indian residents
in Alberta] G. Legge. il Macleans 94:36 Je 15
'81

### Legal status, laws, etc.
*See* Indians of North America—Government
relations

### Medicine
*See also*
Medicine men

### Mines and mineral resources
Indian tribe snares a rich mineral deal [lease
agreement to develop molybdenum mine on
land owned by Colville Confederated Tribes
of Washington State] Bus W p21-2 F 9 '81
Mining contract caves in on AMAX [molybdenum
mine on tribal lands of Colville Confederated
Indian Tribes in eastern Washington] il Bus W
p36 D 7 '81
Navajo mineral swindle: wheeling and dealing
on the reservation [Interior Department vs
lawyer N. Littell] M. Miller and others por
USA Today 109:56-60 My '81
New hope on the reservations. J. Cook. il map
Forbes 128:108-15 N 9 '81

Portrait(s)

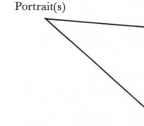

### Missions
*See* Missions

### Museums
About and by Indians [views of G. Horse Capture, curator of Plains Indian Museum, Buffalo
Bill Historical Center, Cody, Wyo.] S. Dallas.
il pors Americana 8:60-5 Ja/F '81

The *Social Sciences Index*[4] indexes the scholarly anthropology, geography, political science, sociology, and social work journals. Here you can get the results of research on such present-day concerns as alcoholism, housing, water rights, the urban Indian, family behavior, etc. *Humanities Index,*[5] while not quite as useful for contemporary information, indexes periodicals in archaeology (e.g., *American Antiquity*, the premier learned journal for New World archaeology); folklore; American and Canadian studies; linguistics; and so on. Historical topics may appear in either index. *Ethnohistory* is indexed in *Social Sciences Index. American Historical Review, Journal of American History, Canadian Journal of History,* and *Canadian Historical Review* are all indexed in *Humanities Index,* so for a thorough review in this field it is necessary to look in both of these titles (which as *Social Sciences and Humanities Index*[6] were one title from 1965 to 1974 and which were preceded by *International Index*[7] which began in 1907).

Other Wilson indexes should be considered depending upon the topic under investigation. Questions on education (both of Indians and about Indians) would lead to *Education Index*[8] which started in 1929. (Another useful index in education, *Current Index to Journals in Education*[9] will be described later along with the abstracting service *Resources in Education*.) Questions on Indian art and on Indian artists would lead to the *Art Index*[10] which also started in 1929. Questions on the Indian in business could lead to *Business Periodicals Index*[11] which began in 1958, and so on. (A pamphlet, *Indexing and Cataloging Services of the H. W. Wilson Company* is available free of charge from the company at 950 University Avenue, Bronx, N.Y. 10452. It lists the company's indexes giving under each title a list of the periodicals covered and sample entries.)

The Wilson indexes have several advantages over other indexes. If a student has ever used *any* index it is likely to be the *Readers' Guide* so the format is familiar. Library of Congress subject headings are used (generally) so one can move from the card catalog to the index and vice versa using the same subject terms, and, pragmatically, since libraries have used the Wilson indexes as buying guides over the years, a student is likely to find the cited journal actually owned by the library.

Another useful and familiar service sure to be in a library of any size is *Public Affairs Information Service Bulletin*[12] which has been indexing books, pamphlets, and government documents, as well as journals, since 1915. It is a good source for legislative information on Indians over the years and a cumulated index covering from 1915 to 1974 makes it easy to search retrospectively.[13] The inclusion of pamphlets is one of its outstanding features. Like the Wilson indexes, it uses Library of Congress subject headings. (It is now online from 1976 on only and will be described further in the chapter on computerized data bases.)

The titles annotated up to now are indexing services which emphasize journals from the United States and Canada. (One exception, the briefly mentioned *International Index*, which was the predecessor of the *Social Sciences Index* and the *Humanities Index*.) There are English-language indexes which pick up articles on Indians which originate from outside North America.

The *International Bibliography of Social and Cultural Anthropology/Bibliographie Internationale d'Anthropologie Sociale et Culturelle*[14] covers journals published all over the world in linguistics, archaeology, area studies, anthropology, and related fields. It is bilingual, English/French, as its title indicates. In the subject index the Indian material here is under the term "Amerindian," unless it pertains to specific tribes in which case, of course, it has the tribe's name as an entry. Like many scholarly indexes this one runs slow. The volume for 1977 was actually published in 1981.

Another index of possible use is the quarterly *Anthropological Index to Current Periodicals in the Museum of Mankind Library (Incorporating the Former Royal Anthropological Institute Library)*.[15] This covers archaeology, ethnomusicology, physical anthropology, ethnography, linguistics, cultural anthropology, and human biology.

Entries here are arranged by region, therefore, the North America section has information on American Indians. There is, unfortunately, no annual cumulated index by subject so this is more of a current-awareness tool than something to use for retrospective searching.

The last major anthropology index is *Anthropological Literature, an Index to Periodical Articles and Essays*.[16] This comes from the Tozzer Library of the Peabody Museum of Archaeology and Ethnology of Harvard University. It has no topic index but does have indexes by ethnic and linguistic groups, archaeological site and culture, and geographic [region].

Another bilingual international index, French/English, is the place to search for scholarly information on Indian languages. It is the *Bibliographie Linguistique/Linguistic Bibliography*[17] published by the Comité International Permanent des Linguistes. This annual started in 1949 but covers work published since 1939. It has no subject index, but its table of contents puts American Indian languages under their "stock" — Macro-Siouan, Macro-Hokan, etc. — sufficient for the serious students who are the only ones likely to use this tool.

The well-known *MLA International Bibliography*[18] published by the Modern Language Association of America is also a source of information on Indian languages in its linguistics section (Look under "American Indian" linguistics.) It furthermore picks up articles on American Indian literature in its General and Miscellaneous section under American Literature I, and it indexes folklore in its folklore section. This folklore section is broken down into topics such as prose narrative; folk poetry; music and dance; folk customs, beliefs and symbolism; material culture; and so on. One must look under the geographic heading "North America" and then under these various rubrics to get at the Indian material.

*MLA* is on-line now from 1970 on and will also be discussed in the on-line data base chapter.

As could be expected from its title, *Religion Index One: Periodicals*[19] is a prime source for articles on missions and on Indian religion. It also picks up articles on mythology, art, language, history, and current Indian social concerns. In its 1979–1980 volume it indexed 263 journals with preference given to journals published in North America and to English-language journals from other countries, "though there is substantive coverage of scholarly journals in Western European languages" (p. iii, 1979–1980 volume).

Many of its articles have abstracts. It is on-line from 1975 to the present in the ATLA Religion Database. (See the on-line chapter.)

And finally there are two offspring of the computer age which large university libraries will have. They are *Social Sciences Citation Index*[20] and *Arts and Humanities Citation Index.*[21] *SSCI* is on-line as *Social Scisearch* and will be described in the on-line data base chapter, but a description is given here for manual users. *AHCI* is available only in the print form.

*SSCI* and *AHCI* are arranged similarly. Both have a citation index, a source index, a corporate index, and a "Permuterm" subject index. The citation index is used to find out who has cited a given article. (You know of one article exactly on the subject you would like to write about. You assume that other writers on this topic will have cited that same article and, if you can find out who they are and what they have written, you will have a good start on a bibliography — this is the purpose of a citation index.)

The source index is equivalent to an author index. The corporate index lists alphabetically by city the author's home organization or school and the Permuterm Subject Index is an alphabetic index arranged by significant words in the title. Thus, one looking for articles on Indian medicine would use the keyword "Indian" and scan down under that word looking for a title which also had the word medicine in it—remembering in this particular example that if the title did not distinguish between Asian Indian and American Indians, the computer will not either and it is up to the eye to rule out the unwanted citation. (Permuterm indexes are also useful if there is only one distinctive word in a title, for example, a tribal name.)

*Social Sciences Citation Index* and *Arts and Humanities Citation Index* both take some work to grasp. Puzzling symbols and up to eight columns of tiny print make this an initially bewildering reference work. Still, its extensive coverage, 900 journals in *AHCI* and 1,500 fully covered in *SSCI* (another 2,800 natural, physical, and biomedical journals are selectively covered for articles in the social sciences) make this a valuable reference tool.

The indexes described so far are currently being published. Some ceased-publication indexes which were serials (i.e., came out at regular intervals) are still important and they are listed here. Also identified here are three one-volume indexes to major United States government serials which concerned Indians.

Four volumes of the *Index to Literature on the American Indian*[22] appeared in the 1970s, (1970, 1971, 1972, and 1973). They were published by the Indian Historian Press which is the publishing arm of the American Indian Historical Society, a nonprofit organization founded in 1964 in San Francisco by tribal leaders and native scholars. These volumes indexed about 120 United States and Canadian journals and also picked up books, government documents, and dissertations. Arrangement is by a mix of geographic (e.g., "Great Basin Indians") and topical subject headings. The subject headings reflected the contemporaneous literature. Thus, the 1973 volume included "civil rights," "fishing and hunting," "genocide," "law and litigation," "water and water rights," and so on as well as headings such as "acculturation," "archaeology," and "dance." Titles were also cited alphabetically by author at the beginning of each section.

Another ceased-publication title which older libraries may still have on their shelves is the *American Indian Index*[23] which began publication in 1953. This mimeographed work was apparently an ambitious attempt to subject-index pages in history journals and in books, such as Bureau of American Ethnology bulletins, Federal Writer's Project guidebooks, histories (e.g., Quaife's *Chicago and the Old Northwest*, 1913), ethnographies (Underhill's *Red Man's America*, 1953) and so on.

Many individuals' names are here (soldiers and agents as well as Indians). Also listed are villages, battles, forts, places, and archeological sites, etc., and topics such as boats, body painting, lice, liquor, sweat (almost two pages of citations), dogs (almost three pages of citations—use of hair in weaving, as food, as hunting aids, to hunt Indians, for religious use), and so on. A sample citation looks like this: "Amherst, Sir Jeffrey (English soldier) advises distribution of smallpox infected blankets to exterminate the Indians (Marquis: *War Chief of the Ottawa* c.1915 p. 7–8)." (Source: *American Indian Index* No. 107, Section 1, 1963, p. 1051.)

Numbers 1–103 (1953–1963) covered the alphabet from A–Z. The alphabet began again with "A" in Number 104 in mid-1963 and got as far as "Ger" in 1968 when publication ceased. The determined, patient, or just plain curious student may find this tool of some use.

Another old index is *A Guide to Articles on the American Indians in Serial Publications, Part I*[24] which covers up to 1934 and lists articles on Indians in 119 serials from 80 organizations including "a majority of the anthropological series issued by American, Canadian and English museums . . . by the American and Canadian governments; . . . published by American colleges and universities; . . . issued by scientific and historical societies; certain scientific and semi-scientific magazines; (and) three memorial or anniversary volumes." This guide is arranged alphabetically by the name of the serial and then simply lists the articles on Indians found in that particular serial, year-by-year. There is no subject or author index.

This is not a first place to search for access to journal articles but could be used if a person knows only that an article appeared in a certain journal (prior, of course, to 1934), wants to trace publishing trends, or simply wants, in effect, to browse title pages on a large number of journals for articles on Indians. The index was initially prepared to locate references on Indians for the library of the Denver Art Museum.

Still another index, this one to pages in books and government reports instead of to journals, is the *Biographical and Historical Index of American Indians and Persons Involved in Indian Affairs*.[25]

It is a reproduction of an information file developed on cards in the library of the Bureau of Indian Affairs. The card file is of names, events (e.g., battles) and topics (e.g., oratory). Each card, and there are more than 200,000, tells where one can find a picture of, or information on, a person or topic. Thus, one can look up an Indian name and see that that person was a signatory to a certain treaty, or look up a soldier's name and see that he was identified in an annual report, and so on. Coverage is primarily of the latter half of the nineteenth century and the first part of the twentieth.

This set is a key to much obscure information on Indians from all walks of life, government employees, missionaries, traders, agents, explorers, etc. It is not an index that would be used by the average undergraduate, but it could be of service to the serious scholar.

And finally, to end this section on retrospective indexes, there are three cumulated indexes to United States government serial publications which have information on Indians. The first is the United States Bureau of American Ethnology's *List of Publications of the Bureau of American Ethnology with Index to Authors and Titles.*[26] This is Bulletin 200, the last of the famous BAE bulletins. It lists the contents of the BAE's *Annual Reports, Bulletins, Publications of the Institute of Social Anthropology, Contributions of North American Ethnology, Introductions,* and miscellaneous publications.

The second is Mamie T. Miller's *Author, Title, and Subject Checklist of Smithsonian Institution Publications Relating to Anthropology.*[27] (This does *not* include the BAE publications covered by the above title.) This work which is indexed by author, title, and subject (the subject having been determined by scanning the titles of the article) covers the *Smithsonian Annual Report, 1846-1941;* the *Annual Report of the U.S. National Museum, 1848-1942; Contributions from the U.S. National Museum Herbarium 1891-1929; Contributions to Knowledge, 1848-1916;* Explorations and Fieldwork, 1927-1940; *Miscellaneous Collections, 1862-1942;* Scientific Series, 1929-1932; *U.S. National Museum Bulletin, 1875-1942;* and the *U.S. National Museum Proceedings, 1878-1942.*

And a third index, limited to the Smithsonian annual reports but covering a longer time span than Miller's is Stemple's *Author-Subject Index to Articles in Smithsonian Annual Reports 1849-1961.*[28] Miller and Stemple both give good access to the old-time reports on the mounds and other Indian antiquities.

While the most pertinent indexes are listed above, the list could be extended almost indefinitely. Questions on general current information, or back to 1851, would lead to the *New York Times Index.*[29] (This title, as well as other newspaper indexes, can be used to ascertain the date of an event which can then be read about in another newspaper which does not have its own index.) A history student would almost certainly use *Writings on American History*[30] and its variously titled predecessors and successors. (See the Harzfeld title cited below for a rundown of these and other index title changes.) A student interested in Indian health would use *Cumulated Index Medicus,*[31] manually or on-line, and one interested in Indians in cities could use *Index to Current Urban Documents*[32] (which has county documents as well as city documents). If the interest were in local Indians there might be an index produced at the local public library or historical society which would be a more appropriate title than any of the indexes listed here. And finally a student of Indians should never forget the quarterly *Catalogue of Government of Canada Publications*[33] and the United States *Monthly Catalog of United States Government Publications.*[34] Actions of the government touch nearly every facet of Indian life — and have since there was a central government — and these government bibliographies document that.

A disadvantage of most manual indexes is that they must be searched year-by-year unless there is a cumulation, for example, that of *PAIS* mentioned above. Some of the book catalogs to be described later can act as cumulations of indexes, and some sets also cumulate indexes to periodicals. *The Combined Retrospective Index Set to Journals in History 1838–1974*[35] is one of these. It indexes "243 English-language periodicals covering all periods and areas in the field of history." It places article titles under a general subject category (e.g., "Indians, American" in Volume VIII) and then simply lists these article titles alphabetically by keyword in the title. Another retrospective index is the *Cumulated Magazine Subject Index 1907–1949,*[36] a cumulation of Faxon's *Annual Magazine Subject Index* which over the years picked up 356 American, Canadian, and English magazines not indexed in other indexing services. It is a good source for articles on local history, art, travel, exploration, and political science journals. (Entries are under "Indians," "Indian, American," "Indians of North America," or "Indians, American," and then by tribe or subject or geographic area.)

The important thing to remember is to pinpoint what aspect of Indian life is being studied and then see if there is an indexing service that provides bibliographic control of that field. Lois Harzfelds's

*Periodical Indexes in the Social Sciences and Humanities: a Subject Guide*[37] describes more than 200 indexes and abstracts. It can serve as a reminder to what is available in printed indexes, but as indexes come and go, the only real way to keep current is to scan the index tables regularly in a large general library.

# 3

## Abstracts

Descriptions of abstracts useful for Indian research follow. (Generally, abstracting services are not as current as indexes as the abstracts take more time to prepare.)

For most purposes, *America: History and Life*[1] and *Resources in Education* are the best abstracting services for Indian-related matters. Their breadth of coverage is staggering. *America: History and Life*, while aimed at the historian and therefore emphasizing history journals also picks up the major American and Canadian studies titles and journals from the disciplines of anthropology, sociology, political science, economics, education, religious studies, popular culture, ethnic studies and the like. It scans more than 2,000 journals in some 38 languages. (The abstracts are always in English). It is currently arranged in four parts: Part A has the abstracts, Part B is an index to book reviews from journals in history and related fields, Part C, "American History Bibliography" arranges the citations from the first two parts (articles, books, and dissertations) alphabetically by author, under the same table of contents as Part A, and Part D is the annual index. This is a computer-produced index which has subject, biographic, geographic, and chronological terms as well as an author approach. Much white space in the format makes this an easy-to-read and attractive reference work—unlike some computer-produced indexes. The basic set covers from 1964 on and a volume "O" covers the periodical literature from 1954 to 1963.

(In 1974 Dwight L. Smith's *Indians of the United States and Canada, a Bibliography*[2] was published.* This put the 1,687 Indian-related abstracts from the *America: History and Life* data bank covering from 1954 to 1972 into one volume which would be a good buy

---

*Volume II of this title was published in 1983. It included another 3128 abstracts of works published primarily since 1972.

25

for a library which does not subscribe to the *America: History and Life* series.)

*AHL* is searchable by computer and will be described further in the data base chapter.

A vast amount of information on American Indians is abstracted in the monthly *Resources in Education*[3] which started in 1966. In early 1982 a computer query showed that there were 7,575 entries in the Educational Resources Information Center (ERIC) data base (*RIE* plus *Current Index to Journals in Education*)[4] which had "American Indian" as either a major or minor "descriptor" (i.e., subject heading). There were also 199 documents with the newer term "Canada Natives." (This data base is searchable either manually or via computer and like *AHL* will be discussed again in the computer chapter.) ERIC is much broader than education and in it one can find material on Indian languages, Indian cultural heritage, federal Indian relationship, school-community relations, bilingual education, Indian values, the aged, and so on, as well as the to-be-expected curriculum guides, annotated bibliographies, teaching methods (about Indians and for Indians). A plus, of course, is that much of the material abstracted is available in the library on microfiche if the library has the ERIC microfiche collection. (About seven hundred institutions in the United States and in Canada had it in 1982.) If the item is not on microfiche, the library may well own it on paper. In any case, ordering information is given. While *RIE* abstracts government documents that fall within its scope, planning studies, papers presented at meetings, and annual reports — the so-called fugitive literature of education — its sister service *CIJE* indexes some 750 magazines representing the "core" periodical literature in the field of education. *CIJE* also indexes important articles regarding education published in those periodicals which fall *outside* the scope of education-oriented literature. It thus covers many more journals than Wilson's *Education Index*, but *Education Index* is still valuable for the prior-to-1969 education literature (*EI*'s coverage began in 1929) and for the other reasons given concerning Wilson indexes.

*CIJE* provides one-or two-sentence notations of the periodical articles which it indexes if such notation is necessary to show the content of the article. As it indexes some foreign-language magazines and many of the lesser-known education publications, a library is not as likely to own all of the titles cited as is the case with the Wilson-indexed journals. Accordingly, one may have to go through interlibrary loan (that is, ask the library to get a free photocopy of the article from another library which owns the journal).

Questions concerning any facet of Indian education can be sent: Attention — American Indian Specialist, ERIC/Clearinghouse on Rural Education and Small Schools, Box 3AP, New Mexico State University, Las Cruces, NM 88003.

Other abstracting services are useful according to the subject being researched. *Psychological Abstracts*[5] since 1927 has provided "non-evaluative" summaries of the world's literature in psychology, and here, under the umbrella index term of "American Indians," you can find many articles on psychology and the Indian. Material since 1967 in this data base is computer-searchable.

Another example of a well-done scholarly tool that should not be overlooked is *GeoAbstracts,*[6] particularly its sections "C," Economic Geography; "D," Social and Historical Geography, and "F," Regional and Community Planning. This service, international in scope, scans about 1,110 journals in geography and related fields and also abstracts some books. Its computer-produced index is of the "keyword" variety, with words also chosen if necessary from the body of the abstract. It should not be ignored by the serious student as it picks up foreign writings and viewpoints on American Indians.

Other useful abstracts are *Social Work Research and Abstracts;*[7] *Language and Language Behavior Abstracts;*[8] and *Women Studies Abstracts.*[9] *Social Work* summarizes articles in about 200 journals on child custody, mental health, the aged, alcoholism, and so on. Its index uses the term "Native Americans." *Language and Language Behavior Abstracts*, computer-searchable since 1973, surveys the world's language periodicals and journals of related disciplines such as anthropology, medicine, information science, and comparative literature, for articles on linguistics and language behavior. *LLBA* uses the terms "North Amerindian languages" and "American Indian" in its index. *Women Studies Abstracts*, using "Indians (North American)" as its indexing term, picks up articles on Indian women.

Of lesser use, generally because of poor indexing practices, is *Abstracts in Anthropology*[10] and *Sociological Abstracts.*[11] *Abstracts in Anthropology* has abstracts from about 80 anthropology journals. (The number varies with each issue.) Entries are arranged in four categories: archaeology, subdivided by region; cultural anthropology, subdivided by topic (arts, ethnohistory, kinship, minorities, psychological anthropology, etc.); linguistics; and physical anthropology. *AIA* has no cumulated index at the end of each year so that one must go issue-by-issue through each volume, and while specific tribal names are in the subject index, there is no overall term such as "Indians of North America" or "Native Americans" to help in identifying articles on American Indians when information on a specific tribe is not necessary.

*Sociological Abstracts*, the expected starting point for scholarly sociological investigations, sometimes uses "Native American" or "American Indian" as its indexing terms, and sometimes it is impossible to puzzle out what term, if any, it uses in the subject index since articles about Indians that appear not to be indexed can be found by scanning the body of the service. As most articles concerning American Indians from a sociological standpoint can be found in easier-to-use services (e.g., *Social Sciences Index*) it may be that only the scholar needing in-depth coverage (foreign-language articles, papers presented at meetings) will want to tangle with *Sociological Abstracts* — at least manually. It is on-line since 1963 and may be searched by computer. (See the computer chapter.)

# 4

## On-line Data Bases

Printed indexes and abstracts which must be searched manually were discussed in previous chapters. It is possible to do bibliographic searching by machine if the printed indexes are in a computer and are therefore machine-readable. This way of compiling a bibliography is called computerized bibliographic searching. To do it, relevant keywords or subject headings — usually called descriptors — are typed into a computer terminal (that is, an electric typewriter or video display unit linked with a computer in which the information from the printed indexing or abstracting service is stored). The results, then, are simply a printout, a computer-printed bibliography, which, like the printed indexes and abstracts, usually does not give the information itself but tells in what journal or book it can be found. (Most data bases provide neither more nor less information than the printed source; they are simply the same service stored in a computer.) While a few libraries have their own holdings on-line, the data bases described here are not tied into any one library. Like the printed services, the computer printout tells you that a source exists. It is not necessarily owned by the library which did the computer search.

The advantages of computerized bibliographic searching are: currency, because the information in the computer *may* be available before the printed index is received by the library; speed, as a data base by its nature is automatically cumulated so that a searcher no longer must go patiently year-by-year through uncumulated printed index volumes; and convenience, as it is obviously quicker and easier to have a computer type the author's name, the journal title, the volume, the date, and the pagination.

Possible disadvantages are: expense, as most libraries must charge for computerized bibliographic searching; and time lost, either in waiting for an interview with the search librarian or in waiting for the results to come. (Searches printed on-line are available at the time the search is done; searches printed off-line, the choice of many libraries because it is cheaper, must come by mail from the vendor's headquarters.)

Some questions, of course, do not lend themselves to computer searching. Much of the older literature in history and anthropology is not yet in a data base as few data bases go back before the mid-1960s.

To take advantage of the benefits of computer searching it is essential to have a well-thought-out strategy. If the service uses a "controlled" vocabulary (subject headings assigned to the material stored in the computer), you and the computer librarian must pay special attention to finding the proper descriptor. Is the term "American Indians" or "Native Americans" or "Amerindian"? If the service has a free-text or natural language approach you must think of synonyms for the subject being researched. Thus, if you want information on aging Indians, you would also search for titles with the words "old" or "aged" or "elderly" or even "senior citizen." All possible variants of a tribal name should also be used. Otherwise, one asking for information on the Maliseet, for example, could miss works using the spelling Malecite. A student wanting information on the Iroquois should also suggest the terms "Iroquoian," "Six Nations," "Five Nations," the names of the constituent tribes, Mohawk, Oneida, Cayuga, and so on and perhaps even the word, "longhouse." This approach is necessary because in many data bases only the words in the title of an article are scanned and if the keyword is not suggested – or is not spelled the way it appears in the title – the sought-for article will not appear on the computer printout. A successful search requires close cooperation with the librarian doing the searching *and some preliminary knowledge on the student's part.*

Computerized bibliographic searching is one of the fastest-changing aspects of the American library scene. New data bases seem to come on-line almost monthly, and data bases already on-line extend their coverage backwards in time as well as forward so that the coverage is ever-changing. The only way to keep up in this field is to talk regularly to the person in charge of data base searching. He or she will receive regular communications regarding changes in coverage, methods of searching, costs, and so on. An ordinary user should pick up any handouts a library has prepared describing data bases available for on-line searching, the charges, and how long it takes to get the results.

Descriptions of data bases, remembering that dates of coverage change frequently, are in several directories which are updated every year or so. Sample titles include Martha E. Williams' *Computer-Readable Bibliographic Data Bases, a Directory and Data Source Book* (Washington, D.C.: American Society for Information Science, 1982); *Directory of On-Line Information Resources*, 8th ed. (Kensington, Md.: CSG Press, 1981); and James Logan Hall and Marjorie J. Brown's *On-line Bibliographic Data Bases: An International Directory*, 2d ed. (London: Aslib, 1981).

These directories generally list the data bases, the subjects covered by each, give the dates of coverage, name the vendor (company which makes the data base available), give the file size, and also give the cost per connect-hour (the usual method of charging).

The introduction to the Hall and Brown book above, pp. xv–xxx, gives a brief and readable overview of on-line searching complete with schematics, graphs, statistics, and a bibliography for further reading.

This chapter describes only some of the data bases useful for American Indian research. Refer to the directories listed above and consult with the computer librarian to see if there are other data bases appropriate to your subject, remembering that Indian information may be a small part of the total records of a data base but still comprise a large part of the literature available on a particular topic. If you do not know which data base is most useful for your topic, the librarian (in libraries which have access to many data bases) can type the topic into the terminal and see which file has the most "hits" on that particular subject. In this way you can zero in on the most appropriate data bank. (There are data bases which cover current news of all subjects, based on newspaper and popular magazine files, but the ones described here are restricted to those which cover specific subjects or disciplines.)

The files here are listed in alphabetical order. For each one, its name is given, its acronym or short name, the printed source it corresponds to* (if one exists), the major subjects covered, the time span covered, the format covered (i.e., whether books, journals, government documents, or audiovisual materials), the number of items in the data base, the indexing method (controlled or free-text); the terms used for American Indians (if a controlled vocabulary), the number of items with this term, and the citation of a typical document.

---

*If there is a printed source, it is wise to scan it to see what subjects are covered and what terms are used. You may even find that a computer search is unnecessary — that you can get sufficient information from a manual search of the printed index.

The indexing method refers to the subject approach. Bibliographic data bases can always be searched by the author's name.

For the sample documents, I have standardized and, in some cases, shortened the actual citation. (Bibliographic form varies widely and wildly in these data bases.)

### America: History and Life

*AHL* is produced by ABC-Clio of Santa Barbara, California. Its print counterpart is also called *America: History and Life*. Its coverage is of journal articles published since 1954 (with coverage of books, book review citations, and dissertations since 1974 as well). For American Indian subjects the coverage is from prehistory to the present — anything written on Indians and published in some 750 U.S. and Canadian journals and 1,250 foreign journals. (The abstracts are always in English.)

There is no controlled vocabulary, thus variant spellings of tribal names (Sac Indians, Sauk Indians) must be suggested and synonyms for the topic being researched suggested as well. Since the words in the abstract of an entry are searched as well as the words in the title, the chances of finding relevant material are better than in the title-only data bases.

There are about 169,000 records in the AHL data base as of early 1983.

A sample entry is: Bray, Robert T. "Bourgmond's Fort D'Orleans and the Missouri Indians." *Missouri Historical Review*. 75, no. 1 (1980): 1–32.

### ASI/American Statistics Index

*ASI* is produced by the Congressional Information Service, Inc. of Washington, D.C. It is *the* source for statistics about United States Indians. Corresponding to the printed *American Statistics Index: A Comprehensive Guide and Index to the Statistical Publications of the U.S. Government,* it covers from 1973 to the present. There is no controlled vocabulary as such, but documents on Native Americans nearly always use the word "Indian" or "Indians."

The total number of items in this data base in early 1983 was 80,000. It is, as its name indicates, limited to United States government publications.

A typical document is: *Royalties: a Report on Federal and Indian Mineral Revenues for 1981, with Summary Data from 1980–1981.* Annual. 1982. 72 p. (United States Geological Survey.)

## *ATLA Religion Database*

The producer of ***RELI*** is the American Theological Library Association of Chicago, Illinois. It covers scholarly, multidisciplinary, and pastoral works about religion, theology, and the Bible in books, journal articles, theses, book reviews, and festschriften. (A festschrift is a volume of essays by several authors honoring a scholar on his birthday or some other anniversary.) Writings on modern-day Indian social concerns — land claims, health services — as well as articles on missions, mythology, Indian spirituality, etc. are cited in this data base. *RELI* corresponds to three printed indexes. They are *Religion Index One: Periodicals* which is on-line from 1975 to the present; *Religion Index Two: Multi-Author Works* which is on-line from 1970 to the present; and *Religion Index Two: Festschriften* which is on-line for the 1960–1969 period.

There are more than 130,000 items in this data base. A sample entry is Dart, John. "Religious Freedom and Native Americans." *Theology Today*. 38 (July 1981): 174–181.

## *BEBA*

***BEBA*** is the acronym for Bilingual Education Bibliographic Abstracts. It is a part of the National Clearinghouse for Bilingual Education (NCBE) data base of Rosslyn, Virginia. NCBE is the only data base in the United States which specializes in bilingual education. Its accessions file lists materials held in selected bilingual education centers throughout the country; its bibliographic file has citations with abstracts to all kinds of works on bilingual and bicultural education particularly those that are not available commercially such as classroom activities, conference proceedings, theses, etc.; and its directory file gives names and addresses of federal agencies, professional organizations, publishers, and individuals engaged in bilingual and bicultural education.

It has more than 5,000 records in its data base which covers generally from 1978 to the present.

Some of this data base's material is also in ERIC.

A typical document is Martin, Jeanette P. *Survey of the Current Study and Teaching of North American Indian Languages in the United States and Canada*. Arlington, Va.: Center for Applied Linguistics, ERIC Clearinghouse on Languages and Linguistics, 1975. 90 p.

## *Child Abuse and Neglect*

***Child Abuse and Neglect*** is produced by the National Center for Child Abuse and Neglect, Children's Bureau, United States Department of Health, Education, and Welfare, Washington, D.C. It contains records of ongoing research project descriptions, bibliographic references (books, periodical literature, government and research reports, and conference proceedings), service program listings, legal references, and audiovisual materials.

It is on-line from 1965 to the present with 12,000 citations as of early 1983.

A sample document is: Baurley, M. E. and M. H. Street. *American Indian Law: Relationship to Child Abuse and Neglect.* Arlington, Va.: Herner and Co. February 1981. 56 p. (Prepared for National Center on Child Abuse and Neglect.)

## CIS

*CIS* comes from the Congressional Information Service, Inc. Washington, D.C. It corresponds to the printed *Index to Publications of the United States Congress* and from 1970 to the present it has indexed the hearings, prints, reports, documents, and other special publications of Congress including specially commissioned studies, legislative analyses, transcripts of testimony from government and public witnesses, and compilations of background material.

In early 1983 it had 160,000 records in its data base. It is searchable by subjects; names; titles; bills, report, and document numbers; and names of committee and subcommittee chairmen.

A typical document in this data base is: "Authorizing the States and the Indian Tribes to Enter into Mutual Agreements Respecting Jurisdiction and Governmental Operations in Indian Country." October 1, 1982. 97–2. 13 p. Senate Report 97–653.

## Educational Resources Information Center (ERIC)

*ERIC* comes from the National Institute of Education, Washington, D.C. It corresponds to the printed *Resources in Education (RIE)* and *Current Index to Journals in Education (CIJE).* Its major subject is education — interpreted very broadly. The monthly *Resources in Education* covers papers presented at meetings, in-house publications, research reports, dissertations, masters theses, government documents, conference proceedings, reference materials, etc. *Current Index to Journals in Education* cites articles from more than 750 education periodicals and also picks up education-related articles appearing in journals of the other disciplines and in the general periodical press. The subjects of the sixteen clearinghouses, which screen and contribute the material to the central ERIC organization, give an idea of the scope of ERIC. The clearinghouses are Adult, Career and Vocational Education; Counseling and Personnel Services; Educational Management; Elementary and Early Childhood Education; Handicapped and Gifted Children; Higher Education; Information Resources; Junior Colleges; Language and Linguistics; Reading and Communication Skills; Rural Education and Small Schools; Science, Mathematics and Environmental Education; Social Studies/Social Science Education; Teacher Education; Tests, Measurement and Evaluation; and Urban Education.

In early 1983 there were approximately 481,000 citations in the data base. Some 7,575 had the descriptor, "American Indians," and 199 had been assigned the newer term "Canada Natives." Other relevant, narrower, terms ERIC uses are "Alaska Natives"; "American Indian Culture"; "American Indian Education"; "American Indian Languages"; American Indian Literature"; American Indian Reservations"; "American Indian Studies'" "Federal-Indian Relationship"; "Nonreservation American Indians"; "Reservation American Indians"; "Rural American Indians"; and "Urban American Indians."

Since it is subsidized by the government, ERIC is the least expensive data base to search. And, as noted earlier, much of the material indexed in *Resources in Education* is owned by the library if it is one of the 700 institutions which subscribes to the ERIC microfiche service.

Pamphlets describing ERIC and its services and giving the addresses of the clearinghouses are available from: Educational Resources Information Center (ERIC), Central ERIC, National Institutes of Education, Washington, D.C. 20208, (202) 254–7934. A guide specific to Indian matters is Ramona T. Sandoval's *How to Search ERIC for American Indian Materials*, 97 p. As of 1979 this was available for purchase from National Educational Laboratory Publishers, Inc., 813 Airport Boulevard, Austin, Texas 78702, Stock No. EC–077, $8.00.

As noted in the chapter on abstracts, questions on any aspect of Indian education can be sent: Attention — American Indian Specialist, ERIC/Clearinghouse on Rural Education and Small Schools, Box, 3AP, New Mexico State University, Las Cruces, New Mexico 88003.

A typical title in the ERIC data base is: *Resolving Discipline Problems for Indian Students: A Preventative Approach*. February 1981.

50 p. ED #197 907 [Available from ERIC Clearinghouse on Rural Education and Small Schools, Box 3AP, NMSU, Las Cruces, N.M. 88003. ($6.90).]

### Exceptional Child Education Resources

*ECER* is produced by the Council for Exceptional Children, Reston, Virginia. Its print counterpart is the quarterly *Exceptional Child Education Resources*. It covers all aspects of the education of handicapped and gifted children from 1966 to the present and includes books, journal articles, teaching materials, and reports. In early 1983 it had 51,000 citations in its data base with some 200 concerning American Indians. Only about one-half of these materials is also in the ERIC data base.

A sample entry is: Johnson, Marilyn J. and others. *Planning Services for Young Handicapped American Indian and Alaska Native Children.* Chapel Hill: North Carolina University, Technical Assistance Development System, 1980. 211 p.

### GPO Monthly Catalog

The *GPO Monthly Catalog* comes from the United States Government Printing Office in Washington, D.C. It is the machine-readable equivalent of the printed *Monthly Catalog of United States Government Publications.* Almost any subject is covered in this data base — agriculture, law, health, religion, history, human rights, safety standards, statistics, energy resource, tax reform, and much more. It is limited to publications of the United States government which are books, journals, reports, fact sheets, studies, maps, handbooks, conference proceedings, census data, Senate and House hearings on private and public bills and laws, and so on. In early 1983 there were 140,000 records in this data base which covered from 1976 on. Some 696 had the subject heading "Indians of North America." (*The GPO Monthly Catalog* uses the *Library of Congress Subject Headings* as its thesaurus.)

A sample document in this data base is: *American Indian Civil Rights Handbook.* 2d ed. Washington, D.C., U.S. Commission on Civil Rights. For sale by the Supt. of Docs. U.S. G.P.O., 1980. 71 p.

### Language and Language Behavior Abstracts

*LLBA* comes from Sociological Abstracts, Inc. of San Diego, California. It corresponds to the printed *Language and Language Behavior Abstracts* covering hearing, learning disabilities, lexicography, linguistics, morphology, nonverbal communication, phonetics, semantics, speech, syntax, typology, and writing in some 1,000 domestic and foreign journals from 1973 to the present. In early 1983 it had 62,000 records in its data base. "North Amerindian languages" and "American Indian" are terms it uses in its annual printed index.

A sample entry is Carlson, Barry F. "Two-Goal Transitive Stems in Spoken Salish." *International Journal of American Linguistics*. 46, no. 1 (January 1980): 21–26.

## Medline

*Medline* is produced by the United States National Library of Medicine, Bethesda, Maryland and corresponds to the printed *Index Medicus, Index to Dental Literature,* and *International Nursing Index.* Its subject is anything in biomedicine in some 3,000 journals published in the United States and 70 other countries. (Since it is limited to journals, government publications as, for example, those of the Indian Health Service must be found in the GPO data base or one of the medical data bases that does pick up documents.) Medline covers from 1966 to the present and in early 1983 had 3,972,000 records of which about 2,000 had the descriptor "Indians, North American." *Medline* uses MeSH (*Medical Subject Headings*) as its thesaurus.

A sample citation: Sievers, M. L. and J. R. Fisher. "Decreasing Incidence of Disseminated Coccidioidomycosis Among Piman and San Carlos Apache Indians." *Chest.* 82, no. 4 (October 1982): 455–460.

## MLA Bibliography

The *MLA Bibliography* data base is produced by the Modern Language Association of America, New York. It contains citations to journal articles, books, symposia, proceedings, and collected works on modern language, literature, linguistics, nonverbal communication, and folklore. Covering from 1970 to the present with over 500,000 records, its print counterpart is the *MLA International Bibliography of Books and Articles on the Modern Languages and Literatures.* It can be searched by a combination of broad descriptors and keywords in the title.

A sample citation: Walle, Alf H. "The Morphology and Social Dynamics of an American Indian Folktale." *Kentucky Folklore Record: a Regional Journal of Folklore and Folklife.* 24 (1978): 74–80.

## NCJRS

*NCJRS* is produced by the National Criminal Justice Reference Service of Rockville, Maryland. It covers law enforcement and criminal justice; courts; corrections; juvenile justice; community crime prevention; and fraud, waste, and abuse in government programs. Research reports; papers, books, articles, and audiovisual presentations are the formats covered. NCJRS uses both a controlled vocabulary and free-text searching. "American Indians" is the descriptor for Native Americans. Other relevant terms include "Indian justice;" "reservation crimes"; "reservation law enforcement"; "tribal court system;" "tribal police"; etc.

NCJRS is on-line from 1972 to the present with a total of 63,000 records.

A sample citation is: Taft, P. B., Jr. "Behind Prison Walls, Indians Reclaim Their Heritage–A New Political and Cultural Awareness Combats the Cycle of Despair." *Corrections Magazine 7*, no. 3 (June 1981): 6–15.

## NTIS

*NTIS* comes from the National Technical Information Service United States Department of Commerce, Springfield, Virginia. Corresponding to the printed *Government Reports Announcement and Index* it covers the technical and scientific reports generated by the United States (and to a lesser extent, state and local) government agencies. Subjects covered include energy, environment, health planning, urban planning, social and biomedical science, etc. In early 1983 it had 957,000 cites covering from 1964 to the present.

A sample citation is Lucero, F. J., Jr. "Energy Development on Native American Lands: Resource and Attitudes, an Interpretive Report on Two Major Indian Conferences of 1980." 1982. 34 p.

## PAIS International

*PAIS International* is the counterpart of the printed *Public Affairs Information Service Bulletin* and *Public Affairs Information Service Foreign Language Index*. It is produced by PAIS, Inc. of New York City, New York. (Public Affairs Information Service is a nonprofit association of libraries based in New York which has been publishing the *PAIS Bulletin* since 1915 and the *Foreign Language Index* since 1972). This data base (the PAIS file is on-line since 1976) covers political science, banking, public administration, international relations, economics, law, social welfare, sociology, social anthropology, and is especially good for public policy issues. The formats included are journals, books, government documents, agency reports, pamphlets, and directories.

In early 1983 it had 204,000 citations in its database.

A sample citation is: Long, J. Anthony and others. "Federal Indian Policy and Indian Self-Government in Canada: an Analysis of a Current Proposal." *Canadian Public Policy.* (Guelph) 8 (Spring 1982): 189–199.

## *PSYCHINFO*

*PSYCHINFO* (formerly Psychological Abstracts) is produced by the American Psychological Association, Washington, D.C. It covers the world's literature in psychology and related disciplines in the behavioral sciences, abstracting articles from more than 900 journals and 1,500 books and technical reports each year.

In early 1983 it had 402,000 citations in its data base which covers from 1967 to present. It has a controlled vocabulary. The term "American Indians" was applied to 595 of these citations.

A sample entry in this data base is: Merkur, Daniel. "The Psychodynamics of the Navajo Coyoteway Ceremonial." *Journal of Mind and Behavior*, 2, no. 3 (Fall 1981): 243–257.

### *Social Scisearch*

*Social Scisearch* is produced by the Institute of Scientific Information in Philadelphia, Pennsylvania, and corresponds to the printed *Social Science Citation Index.* It indexes 1,000 social science journals from around the world and also picks up articles on the social sciences from 2,200 other journals in the natural, physical, and biomedical journals. It also includes some monographs.

Social Scisearch is searchable by significant words in the title (which means that the title of an article must be descriptive of its content for this approach to work). It is also possible to search by the author's cited references.

This data base covers from 1972 to the present and in early 1983 had 1,770,000 records in its data base.

A sample citation from this data base is : McCool, D. "Voting Patterns of American Indians in Arizona." *Social Science Journal.* 19, no. 3 (1982): 101–113.

### *Sociological Abstracts*

*Sociological Abstracts* comes from Sociological Abstracts, Inc. of San Diego, California. It abstracts sociology literature from some 1,200 journals worldwide; cites the book reviews in these journals; and also abstracts papers presented at professional meetings.

*Sociological Abstracts* is on line from 1963 to the present with more than 127,000 citations.

A sample citation: Olson, Mary B. and Ada E. Deer. "Through the 'Safety Net': the Reagan Budget Cuts and the American Indian with a Focus on the Menominee Tribe." 1982. (This is an example of a citation to a paper presented at a professional meeting. In this case, the paper was presented at a meeting of the Rural Sociological Society. The complete paper is available from the Sociological Abstracts Reproduction Service at $0.20 per page plus $1.00 search and postage. Length of paper: 33p.)

# 5

# Library Catalogs

Book catalogs are composed of photographed copies of the cards in a library's catalog bound into book form. Using them a researcher many miles away from the specialized library itself may become aware of the existence of a book or journals article. The book can then be borrowed through interlibrary loan or a photocopy of the journal article requested.

No data base has the historic depth of the great collections recorded in these volumes. Their use distinguishes the scholar, who needs a comprehensive bibliography for a dissertation or book, from the student who simply needs a selective bibliography for a term paper.

(A "dictionary" catalog means that you can look up a work by author, or by title, or by subject, and that these are all filed in one alphabet. "Analytics" means that periodical articles as well as parts *in* books are listed in the catalog.)

The first catalog described here is the *Dictionary Catalog of the Department [of the Interior] Library.*[1] This library was founded in 1949 from the collections of the Bureau of Biological Survey (established in 1885); the Fish and Wildlife Service (established in 1871); the Bureau of Indian Affairs (1824); the Bureau of Mines (1910); and the Office of the Solicitor (1849). It also includes material from the Bureau of Land Management and the National Park Sevice.

Its catalog includes archival and unpublished material (i.e., conference proceedings, mimeographed government reports), periodical articles and many books covering such subjects as public land policy, history of irrigation, government relations with the Indian tribes, Indian constitutions and tribal laws, reports on resources of the United States territories, and biographies, diaries and letters of people active in the building of the Old West. There is also some material of Canadian interest.

Library of Congress subject headings are used, and to get an idea of the amount of information here, citations under "Indians of North America" cover 157 pages in volumes 15 and 16 of the original set and are in like proportion in the appropriate volumes in each of the four supplements.

The *Dictionary Catalog of the Edward E. Ayer Collection of Americana and American Indians*[2] in the Newberry Library was published in 1961 when the collection had 90,000 "pieces."

It includes pre-Columbian discovery material, early geographies, colonization, missionary labors, Northwest coast explorations, Arctic voyages, trans-Mississippi explorations, Indian wars, captivities, and the archaeology and ethnology of all the Indian tribes of both North and South America. There are many rare books and old government documents – a wealth of material.

The first supplement (1970) and the second supplement (1980) together recorded the addition of another 19,000 books, and the second supplement also fully catalogs the noted Everett D. Graff collection of Western Americana of more than 4,800 titles. The 1980 supplement also "reflects a new policy in the Ayer collection, which during the past ten years has attempted to acquire copies of every dissertation on the American Indian."

While cataloging practices are not described in either the introduction to the basic set or to the supplements, they appear to follow standard Library of Congress headings fairly closely.

There are occasional analytics.

The *Dictionary Catalog of the American Indian Collection of the Huntington Free Library and Reading Room*[3] is of the Library for the Museum of the American Indian, Heye Foundation in the Bronx, New York.

It catalogs over 35,000 volumes concerning the "anthropology, art, history and current affairs of all the Native Peoples of the Western Hemisphere."

The catalog is of books, periodicals, periodical articles, and Indian newspapers. It is arranged by a modified Library of Congress classification scheme. (For example, the Library of Congress heading "Indians of North America – New York" is changed to "New York State Indians," and many general headings begin "Indians of North America" which is frequently abbreviated as "I. N. A.".)

This is a wonderful tool to a wonderful collection.

More than 100 years old, the Tozzer Library of the Peabody Museum of Archaeology and Ethnology at Harvard University is the premier anthropology library in the world, and it specializes in New World ethnology and archaeology. It comprised about 136,000 volumes in 1981. Its catalog, called since 1979, *Catalogue of the Tozzer Library of the Peabody Museum of Archaeology and Ethnology, Harvard University,*[4] is an author and subject index to these books and pamphlets and, since 1910, to articles in periodicals and collected works, such as *festschriften*, as well.

The author catalog, besides listing works *by* author also provides biographical and critical material *on* an author. (Obituaries, for example, are indexed here.)

The subject catalogs use Tozzer's own system of subject headings which are of three types, "topics, geographic areas, and human groups defined linguistically, socially, geographically and politically" (p. vii, Volume I, *Third Supplement*). *The reader is urged to read this introduction before trying to use the Peabody via subject.*

Much general American Indian material is filed under a heading which begins "North America" and is then subdivided by region and/or topic, (e.g., "North America — Plains — Archaeology"), but material can also be found by specific topic (e.g., "linguistics") or tribal name — which is first listed under stock (i.e., Mohawk is under "Iroquoian," Mandan is under "Siouian," and so on).

This catalog is a great retrospective bibliography for information on peoples of the New World. There are, however, many quirks in the subject scheme and until you are familiar with the subject headings, it is not a quick place to find information by topic. (If an author of an article or book is known, of course, the approach is quite straightforward.)

In 1981 *The Tozzer Library Index to Anthropological Subject Headings*[5] was published. The subject headings in this list more adequately reflect present-day anthropology. Only a few of these new subject headings, however, appear in the fourth supplement so its effect will not really be noticeable until the fifth supplement appears.

*The Catalog of Folklore, Folklife and Folk Songs,* Second Edition[6] provides a subject approach to the 36,000 volumes in the John G. White Department of Folklore, Orientalia, and Chess of the Cleveland Public Library. This collection was begun in 1899 and is "comprehensive in scope and international in coverage" (p. iii).

Arrangement is by Library of Congress subject headings and eighty-two pages in this three-volume set are taken up with subject headings that start "Indians of North America." The LC subject heading "Indians of North America — Legends" is changed to "Indians of North America—Folk-lore and Legends" and "Indians of North America—Religion and Mythology" is inexplicably changed to "Indians of North America—Mythology and Religion." These two headings apply to a large number of the entries here.

In 1961 the *Dictionary Catalog of the History of the Americas Collection, the Research Libraries of the New York Public Library*[7] was issued in twenty-eight volumes. In this, a great catalog, to a truly great collection, the information on Indians is filed under "Indians, N.A." (i.e., North America). This heading is subdivided by topic, for example, "Indians, N.A.—Education"; by tribe, "Indians, N.A.—Tribes—Comanche"; or by regional area, "Indians, N.A.—Regional areas—Canada." Periodical articles are indexed in this set as well as books (but to a lesser extent in the supplement published in 1973).

Greenwood Publishing Corporation has also published book catalogs of some of America's great libraries. They include *Catalog of the Books in the American Philosophical Society Library*[8] which is especially strong in American Indian linguistics (look under the term "Indian languages" for the various phrases they use); the *Subject Catalog of the Library of the State Historical Society of Wisconsin*[9] which has 230 pages of citations which start "Indians of North America" and which has a separate volumes cataloging its pamphlets by subject; and the American Antiquarian Society Library which has *A Dictionary Catalog of American Books Pertaining to the 17th through 19th Centuries*[10] and whose collections of American books, pamphlets and broadsides through 1820 are preeminent.

And finally, to conclude this chapter on book catalogs, there is the *Subject Catalog—Library of Congress*[11] which since 1950 has recorded, by subject, the books, pamphlets, periodicals and other serials, maps and atlases received and cataloged by the Library of Congress.

The subject heading used here is, naturally, "Indians of North America."

# 6

# Handbooks, Encyclopedias, Dictionary

## HANDBOOKS AND ENCYCLOPEDIAS

The indexes, abstracts, book catalogs, and computerized data bases described in the previous chapters are one kind of reference tool. In effect, they tell where to go to find information. The handbooks, encyclopedias, and dictionary described in this chapter are a different kind of tool. They contain the information within themselves. These kinds* of books are the keystones of a library's reference department, and for Indian study Frederick Webb Hodge's two-volume *Handbook of American Indians North of Mexico*[1] is the stable reference point from which all Indian research begins. It covers "stocks, confederacies, tribes, biographies of Indians of note, sketches of their history, archaeology, manners, arts, customs and institutions . . . ," and its "references form practically a bibliography of the tribe for those who wish to pursue the subject further" (Preface). Published in 1907 and 1910, these two volumes remain in print today.

In 1913 the material relevant to Canada in Hodge's work was extracted and put into the *Handbook of Indians of Canada*.[2] For the Canadian *Handbook* the spelling was changed to conform to English usage and articles pertaining to Canadian treaties, the Canadian Department of Indian Affairs and Canadian Indian Reserves were inserted. New maps were also supplied. This book was reprinted in 1969.

---

*The term handbook which was originally used for a work providing miscellaneous bits of information in a book small enough to be held in one hand, now includes reference works almost indistinguishable from subject encyclopedias. A subject encyclopedia is an encyclopedia which focuses on one subject unlike the general encyclopedias such as *Americana* and *Britannica* which cover all branches of knowledge. A subject dictionary means simply that the information on the topics (in this case Indian tribes) is arranged in dictionary fashion, that is, in alphabetical order.

Another helpful reference book for quick identification of tribal names and geographic locations is John R. Swanton's 1952 *Indian Tribes of North America*.[3] Swanton is a state-by-state compendium on Indian tribes giving the meaning of their names, their population, their history, "connection in which they have been noted," linguistic stock, village names and locations. This book, which also covers Canada, the West Indies, Mexico, and Central America has maps, a long bibliography, and a detailed index.

Reflecting the scholarship of the last sixty years is the new *Handbook of North American Indians*[4] to be published in twenty volumes by the Smithsonian under the general editorship of William C. Sturtevant. Four volumes are so far in print. They are the *Subarctic* (v. 6);[5] *California* (v. 8);[6] the *Southwest* (v. 9);[7] and *Northeast* (v. 15).[8] There will be two volumes for the Southwest. Volume 9 is on the Pueblo peoples. Volume 10 will be on non-Pueblo peoples.

To quote from p. xii of the California volume, this set is "planned to give an encyclopedic summary of what is known about the prehistory, history, and cultures of the aboriginal peoples of North America who lived to the north of the urban civilizations of central Mexico." Topics of the other volumes are: Volume 1, the introduction which gives general descriptions of anthropological and historical methods and sources and summaries for the whole continent on social and political organization, religion, and the performing arts; Volume 2, Indians and Eskimos in contemporary society; Volume 3, environment, origins, and population; Volume 4, history of Indian-white relations; Volume 5, the Arctic; Volume 7, Northwest Coast; Volume 11, the Great Basin; Volume 12, the Plateau; Volume 13, the Plains; Volume 14, the Southeast; Volume 16, technology and visual arts; volume 17, languages; Volumes 18 and 19, the biographical dictionary; and Volume 20, the index.

From this set it is possible to buy any one volume, unlike most encyclopedias which are for sale only as sets.

Judging from the four volumes now in print this set will be profusely illustrated with black and white photographs, maps, and drawings. The articles, by archaeologists, anthropologists, historians, geographers, linguists, and others (few of whom are Indians) are scholarly and have extensive bibliographies, yet they are written so that the interested layperson can understand them. They will appeal to both browser and scholar and in the years to come will be the new starting point for Indian study. In the library, these books, with their handsome light gray binding with red band imprinted in gold, will stand side by side with the scuffed olive green *Bureau of American Ethnology Bulletins* and *Reports*, many of which are still available from the reprint publishers and which the new *Handbook* will supplement but never replace.

For a different audience entirely — junior high-and high-school students or those who simply like their facts in shorter doses — is Scholarly Press's *Encyclopedia of Indians of the Americas*.[9] This title started in 1974 as a projected twenty-volume set to cover both North and South America. As of 1982, only six volumes had appeared. The first volume, bright and colorful with many Indian contributors, was designated "Conspectus. Chronology." The Conspectus had articles on Indian art, Indians of Canada, reverence for the environment, the American Indian image (by Vine Deloria), and so on. The Chronology covers from 25,000 B.C. to 1974 A.D., (and should be used with caution as some authorities do not agree with it). Typical entries from the second volume "A to Assin" are agriculture, allotment policy, Archaic stage, and the like, and the third volume "Assu to Calc" includes entries on athletics, ball games, basketry, bows and arrows, etc. The fourth volume "Calc to Colo" includes captivities, ceramics, child rearing, etc.; the fifth, "Colo to Flat," has articles on communication (including sign language), dance, dwellings, and more; and the sixth, "Flat to Hyda" covers flutes, forts, games, horses, etc. There are also entries for noted Indians, living or dead, as well as for tribes whose names fall into these parts of the alphabet. Pictures of present-day Indians are used where appropriate — Choctaw schoolchildren in Mississippi playing stickball for example. Unlike the first volume, which had many illustrations in color, the following volumes' illustrations, while plentiful, are all in black and white.

There are no bibliographies at the end of an article citing sources or giving suggestions for further reading (even though many of the articles are signed by recognized authorities), thus, despite the name of the publisher, this set is popular, not scholarly. Still, as there is a place for an encyclopedia like this with short, clearly written entries and many illustrations, it is hoped that the publisher can complete the set.*

---

*This publisher has encountered legal difficulties and caution should be exercised in purchasing this set and especially in prepaying for further volumes.

An authoritative source of background information on present-day Indians in the United States is Edward Spicer's long entry on American Indians in the one–volume *Harvard Encyclopedia of American Ethnic Groups.*[10] Noting that tribes vary in size from the Navajos of Arizona and New Mexico, who number more than 160,000, to the Chumash of California and the Modoc of Oklahoma who have less than 100 tribal members, Spicer gives information on the larger, still-extant tribes. For each group he gives a mini-history, tracing its movements through the country since the arrival of the white man, naming and dating the most relevant treaties, battles, and historic events, and concluding with the tribe's present language, social, economic, religious, and statistical (based on 1970 figures) situation.

The essay, which is a masterful summary of information on contemporary Indians, ends with sections on urban Indians and on federal policy toward Indians.

Two outline maps accompany the article. One locates Indian tribes where they were in 1600 and the other gives their primary location as of 1970.

## DICTIONARY

Barbara Leitch's *Concise Dictionary of Indian Tribes of North America*[10] is just that. In essays one to five pages long she gives information on the geographic location, social organization, economics, religion, and language of about 280 of the larger tribes. Each essay cites one or two, occasionally as many as five, standard, older books on the tribe under discussion so that a student would know where to look for more information.

The end papers have maps of Indian-language groups, culture areas, and Indian lands and communities (present-day), and the book is illustrated with black-and-white photographs and drawings from the Bureau of Indian Affairs, Smithsonian Institution, Library of Congress, and the like and includes some of the famous Edward S. Curtis pictures.

This is a good, useful, ready-reference book.

# 7

## Directories, Catalogs, and Dissertation Sources

Directories list people, organizations, associations, institutions, and so on, in an alphabetical or classified arrangement usually also giving addresses and brief descriptive information. Two of the directories described here are also both calendar and fact book, giving the dates of semi-regular events such as powwows and providing small bits of statistical information (e.g., tribal population figures).

Identified here, then, are biographical directories; all-purpose directories; catalogs of books in print, of periodicals, and of films; and directories of reservations, museums, and colleges. The best sources for finding dissertations on American Indians are also given.

### DIRECTORIES AND CATALOGS

For biographical information on contemporary people there are *Indians of Today*[1] and the *Reference Encyclopedia of the American Indian.*[2] *Indians of Today* has brief sketches of 373 Indian men and women and the *Who's Who* volume of the *Reference Encyclopedia of the American Indian* (volume 2) gives biographical notes on Indians (as well as on non-Indians concerned with Indian affairs — anthropologists, historians, museum curators, etc.). Additionally, the *Encyclopedia of Indians of the Americas* has information on living Indians as have several of the titles in Part 2, the annotated bibliography section following. (See the categories for authors, autobiography, biography, and literature.) Biographical information is in the *Handbook of American Indians North of Mexico* and will be in volume 18 and 19 of the new *Handbook of North American Indians*.

The first volume of the *Reference Encyclopedia of the American Indian*, which is not really an encyclopedia but a book of lists, gives addresses and often a one-or-two-sentence description of government agencies, associations (of Indians and for the study of

Indians), museums, monuments and parks, libraries, reservations, tribal councils, urban Indian centers and schools. It also lists college courses, audiovisual aids and audiovisual distributors, magazines and periodicals (on or published by Indians), government publications, and books on Indian subjects.

As much of the information given here—personnel in government agencies, addresses, college course offerings, book prices—is the kind that changes rapidly, this volume should be used with this in mind, a caution which applies to all of these directories.

A better directory, because it is more current, is the *Native American Directory, Alaska, Canada, United States*.[3] Despite occasional errors and omissions, this is presently the best address book, phone book, and calendar of events for native North America. For the United States, addresses and phone numbers of Native American tribal offices are given, federally recognized tribes and bands are listed as are reservations, rancherias, and pueblos. (These latter have population figures.) Population figures (1980) are also given for Indians, Eskimos, and Aleuts by state. There are addresses for the state offices of Indian Affairs, for national Indian organizations (with one or two sentences describing their purpose), Indian-owned museums (and other museums with major collections on Indians), boarding schools operated by the BIA, schools contracted to Indians for operation, Indian community colleges, urban Indian centers, Indian Health Service urban projects, craft guilds and cooperatives, dance groups, newspapers and magazines, radio and television programs, directories for locating native American Indians and Indian products, Indian events (powwows, rodeos, craft shows, etc.), Indian-owned stores (and non-Indian stores which have "excellent examples of traditional native art"), dealers in antique Indian art, dates for Navajo rug auctions, and more.

Similar information is given in separate sections for Alaska and Canada. (The Canadian section also lists "raw craft suppliers," education and friendship centres, and native women's associations as well as the to-be-expected native, Metis, nonstatus Indian, and Inuit associations.) This section also has a long list of the Canadian reserves with their acreage noted.

For the events an approximate date is given (e.g., World Eskimo Indian Olympics, July 4th weekend, University of Alaska, Fairbanks,Alaska), and for any event listed the editor, Fred Snyder, suggests that the Chamber of Commerce or sponsoring tribe or organization be contacted to verify the date.

The publisher's address is P.O. Box 5000, San Carlos, AZ 85550-0301, phone (602) 475-2229.

An older title similar to the *Native American Directory* is the *American Indian Reference Book*.[4] This is another compilation of lists of tribes (alphabetically by state and by tribal name); reservations, rancherias, and villages; cities with large Indian populations; industrial parks; Indian schools; BIA field offices; powwows, festivals, and other annual events; Indian organizations; craft shops; radio stations and periodicals; commissioners of Indian affairs (with date appointed); audiovisual materials (with addresses where to write); museums with outstanding Indian collections; and so on.

Also given are one-line identifications of "Indians of the Past," Indian population figures, and books on Indian-related subjects.

### Books in Print

The annual *Subject Guide to Books in Print,*[5] which began in 1957, lists by subject books available for purchase in the United States.

Under the heading, "Indians of North America," and its many subdivisions, are, in the 1982–1983 volume, forty-seven four-column pages listing books on Indians — the size of the list reflecting the fascination Indians still have for American citizens.

Ordering information, price, and publisher are given in this list which includes many of the old standards republished by the reprint companies.

Bookstores, most medium-sized libraries, and all large libraries will have these volumes in their reference collection.

An equivalent title for Canada is *Canadian Books in Print, Subject Index.*[6] This annual began in 1973.

These two titles may be used to update the lists found in the *Reference Encyclopedia of the American Indian* and the *American Indian Reference Book*. The entries are not annotated, but they are current.

### Periodicals

Periodicals published by Indians, in the past and at present, are listed in *Native American Periodicals and Newspapers, 1828–1982*[7]. This work has 1,164 entries, plus cross-references, and is arranged alphabetically by title with subject, editors, publishers, geographic, catchword/subtitle, and chronological indexes.

A selection guide which covers periodicals of all kinds, including Indian titles, is Katz's *Magazines for Libraries*[8] now in its fourth edition. Since the second edition of 1972 this work has had a chapter describing from twenty to forty Canadian and American Indian publications. (Some editions also list another twenty to thirty titles without giving annotations.)

## Films

*Native Americans on Film and Video*[9] is a catalog of approximately 400 films and videotapes produced primarily between 1970 and 1981 (although some early film classics made before 1940 and anthropological projects from the 1960s which record traditional lifestyles are also included).

The catalog gives for each film or videotape, date of production, running time, language spoken (if other than English), distributors(s), and a paragraph description often with a suggested reference for further reading on the film's subject.

Some of the films here are ethnographic documentaries, some are first-person accounts by individuals describing their own Native American customs and way of life, some cover social and political issues in a news reportage style, and some are fictional. A few are Native-made.

The catalog also has a section listing twenty special film collections which have visual resources on native Americans (examples: American Museum of Natural History, New York; Center for Great Plains Studies, Lincoln, Nebraska; Glenbow Institute, Calgary, Alberta); a resource section which gives names, addresses, and descriptions of media centers, film festivals, and national film organizations concerned with Native American films and videos; a list of distributors; and a short bibliography.

(Nearly all general catalogs, of course, will list some films on Indian subjects.)

## Reservations

For authoritative, brief information on the United States reservations the basic source is *Federal and State Indian Reservations and Indian Trust Areas.*[10] This large paperback published by the U.S. Department of Commerce lists the native villages in Alaska with their populations and then lists Indian reservations by state. For each reservation, population, acreage, and land status (i.e., tribal-owned, government-owned, and/or allotted) are given. This information is followed by a paragraph each on history; culture; government; tribal economy; climate of the reservation; transportation; availability of water, sewage, and health facilities; and vital statistics including labor force and education of the population.

A similar title from Canada is the *Schedule of Indian Reserves and Settlements of Canada.*[11] This government publication lists in tabular form the Indian reserves and settlements, states the names of the Indian bands for whose use and benefit they have been set apart, gives the geographical location (including latitude and longitude so that National Topographical system maps may be ordered), and also gives acreage.

The book is in three parts: part 1 has reserves and settlements alphabetically by province, part 2 lists bands by region, and part 3 is a national summary by province of the number of Indian bands, reserves, settlements, and appropriate reserve acreages.

Population figures are not given nor are any other historical or social data.

Reservations are also listed in the *Reference Encyclopedia of the American Indian,* the *Native American Directory,* and the *American Indian Reference Book.*

## Museums

There are over one hundred museums in North America operated by Native Americans. A spiral-bound *Directory of North American Indian Museums and Cultural Centers*[12] lists and describes the collections, programs, special events, research facilities, publications, hours, etc. of twenty-three of these Indian-run institutions in the United States and Canada. It also gives the addresses of twenty-one other established Indian museums and of nine "in the formative stage."

Pages 38–39 have "Suggested Guidelines for Museums in Dealing with Requests for Return of Native American Materials."

The North American Indian Museums Association was established in 1978. Its address is c/o George Abrams, Seneca-Iroquois National Museum, P.O. Box 442, Salamanca, N.Y. 14779, phone (716) 945–1790.

Other museums which have noted Indian-related collections, not necessarily operated by Native Americans, are listed in the *Reference Encyclopedia of the American Indian*, the *Native American Directory,* and the *American Indian Reference Book.*

## Colleges

The *Directory of Hispanic and American Indian Higher Education Programs*[13] is meant primarily for students who are Hispanic or Indian. It gives information on Hispanic and American Indian education programs available at mainland United States, Puerto Rican, and Alaskan schools. The entry for each school gives enrollment figures, fees, kind of housing available (off campus or on campus) and describes the support services (counseling and guidance, tutoring assistance, financial aid, bilingual counselors, day care availability, Indian and Hispanic clubs and organizations, community resources, and so on) as well as describes the projects and programs that may be of special interest to Hispanic and American Indian students. For each such program the name, address, and phone number of a contact person is given.

There is an index by state and by the name of each special program (examples: American Indian studies, bilingual education, clerical/secretarial, health careers, Hispanic studies, medical sciences, etc.).

Tables in the appendix identify 19 schools which each have over 275 American Indian students enrolled (based on 1978-1979 figures).

About 350 institutions ranging from small community colleges and denominational schools to large state and private universities are included.

Colleges which have courses *on* the American Indian are also listed in the *Reference Encyclopedia of the American Indian. The College Blue Book,*[14] in its Volume I, *Degrees Offered by College and Subject,* is a regularly updated source of colleges which offer degrees in Indian study. (Look under both "Indian" and "Native" to find appropriate courses.)

## DISSERTATIONS

For questions on dissertations on American Indians, Dockstader's *American Indian in Graduate Studies*[15] is the basic work. Part One covers 1890-1955 and Part Two covers 1955-1970. Together they list 7,446 dissertations and masters theses from 274 different schools in the United States, Canada, and Mexico. (Papers designated "practicum" or "project" as distinguished from theses, are also included in Part Two if they are housed in the reporting institution's library.) Occasional comments clarify the topic or identify the tribes discussed if that information is not apparent from the title.

For the 1971-1975 period, Nickerson's *Native North Americans in Doctoral Dissertations*[16] lists another 500 dissertations.

To update these lists, *Comprehensive Dissertation Index, 1861-1972*[17] and its supplements is searchable manually or via computer.

Dissertations were also listed in *Index to Literature on the American Indian.*

(The Newberry Library of Chicago presently has a policy of acquiring a copy of each dissertation on American Indians as it appears.)

# 8

# Archives and Government Documents

## ARCHIVES

Archives are the records which have enduring value of a government agency or other organization or institution. Described here are several titles pertaining to government archives, but the serious researcher should remember that associations, schools, churches, and even families may also have archives with Indian material. The *National Union Catalog of Manuscript Collections*[1] is the principal tool for finding archival manuscript collections in the United States. For Canada, the *Union List of Manuscripts in Canadian Repositories*[2] is the major work.

The National Archives of the United States consists of the permanently valuable records of the federal government. Kept in the National Archives Building in Washington, D.C., and in the Washington National Records Center in Suitland, Maryland, and eleven regional federal archives and record centers located in Waltham, Massachusetts; Bayonne, New Jersey; Philadelphia, Pennsylvania; Atlanta, Georgia; Chicago, Illinois; Kansas City, Missouri; Fort Worth, Texas; Denver, Colorado, San Francisco, California; Los Angeles, California; and Seattle, Washington are about 1,300,000 cubic feet of records.

The most pertinent aid to Indian study in these archives is Edward Hill's *Guide to Records in the National Archives of the United States Relating to American Indians.*[3]

With Hill's guide, the researcher can find, in this great mass of paper, photographs, maps, films, and recordings, the materials that deal with American Indians (including Indians who lived in the former colonies and those who lived along the boundaries of Canada and Mexico and who had relations with the United States).

In the book, pre-federal records are described first. Then come the general records of the U.S. government, chiefly treaties, followed

by the records of the Office of the Secretary of the Interior and
other agencies of the Department of the Interior (in which the Bureau of Indian Affairs has been since 1849), the War Department
records, the Department of the Navy records, the records of Congress and legislative agencies, court records, presidential agencies,
other government, and finally, nongovernment sources.

Most of these records are readily available. A few have some re-
strictions of access so that before traveling any distance to visit a depository, researchers should write and describe as exactly as possible
their subject or interest and the records which they wish to use.

Carmelita S. Ryan's "The Written Record and the American
Indian: the Archives of the United States,"[4] gives a clear idea of
what to expect to find and what *not* to expect to find in the National Archives on Indians and Oliver W. Holmes' chapter
"Indian-related Records in the National Archives and Their Use:
Observations over a Third of a Century," is another fine description of the archival material. This latter citation is one of a
number of illuminating papers in *Indian-White Relations, a Persistent Paradox,*[5] the published proceedings of the National Archives
Conference on Research in the History of Indian-White Relations.

The address of the National Archives is: National Archives
and Records Service, 8th St. and Pennsylvania Ave. N.W.,
Washington, D.C. 20408. They will send a leaflet, "A Researcher's
Guide to the National Archives" free on request.

For Canada, the basic finding aid is the *General Inventory
Series. No. 1 Records Relating to Indian Affairs. (RG 10).*[6] In this
the introduction notes that "The records relating to Indian Affairs
date from 1677 until the present. Included are documents created
by the old British Indian Department, various colonial administra-
tions, and the several branches and departments responsible for
Indian Affairs under federal authority after Confederation. These
records reflect the variegated activities connected with the administration of Indian matters, including the early role of Indians in
military strategy; the negotiation of treaties; reserve land sales and
timber disposal; the provision of educational facilities and administration of trust funds; as well as planning and supervision of
agricultural and industrial projects on reserves" (p. vii). Generally,
records over thirty years old are available for research. The address
of the Public Archives of Canada is: 395 Wellington St., Ottawa,
Canada K1A ON3.

## GOVERNMENT DOCUMENTS

Government documents are publications printed at the expense of a government or published by the authority of a government. An entire book could be written — and probably will be someday — on the the United States publications on the American Indian. Michael Tate in his "Studying the American Indian Through Government Documents and the National Archives"[7] introduces and critiques the guides to Indian material, including the classic documents indexes of the nineteenth century that provide an "open sesame" to the wealth of information in the older government publications; the newer cumulated indexes which cover up to 1975; and, most basic of all, the ongoing *Monthly Catalog of United States Government Publications.* He also describes some collections of source material relevant to Indians — the *American State Papers, Territorial Papers,* and so on — and, as the title indicates, discusses aids to archival research.

Tate's "Red Power: Government Publications and Rising Indian Activism of the 1970s"[8] is a long (more than fifty items are cited) bibliographic essay on the Indian-related government documents published during the prolific decade of the 1970s. Especially mentioned and discussed are titles on education, health care, resource development (mineral and water concerns and agriculture), employment opportunities (or lack thereof), civil rights and jurisdictional problems, administrative problems in general, including the Indian Claims Commission Final Report, and regional and general studies.

Reflecting that some of these documents are critical of the government itself, Tate places them in the social context of the seventies.

These two articles are a fine overview of this body of literature; nevertheless, a first-time user of government documents would be well advised to introduce himself or herself to the government documents librarian, describe the topic of interest, and ask for help.

# Part 2

# *Annotated Bibliography Alphabetically by Topic*

### Agriculture*

Edwards, Everett E., and Wayne D. Rasmussen. *A Bibliography on the Agriculture of the American Indians*. U.S. Department of Agriculture. Miscellaneous Publications, number 447. Washington, D.C.: GPO, 1942.

"It is estimated that four-sevenths of the total agricultural production of the United States . . . consists of economic plants that were domesticated by the Indian and taken over by the white man. The extent of the debt to the Indian is emphasized when we recall that the white man has not reduced to cultivation a single important staple during the 400 years he has dominated the New World" (p. 1).

Printed in 1942 (and sold at that time for $0.15) this fine, detailed bibliography has more than 800 entries (some annotated) on North and South American Indian agriculture.

Sections include: comprehensive references; agriculture of particular regions and tribes; specific crops and animals (corn, cotton, maple sugar, potatoes, tobacco, wildrice, etc.); agriculture on Indian reservations in the United States; and uncultivated plants (food and industrial plants and medicinal plants).

Titles are mostly English, but there are a few in French, Spanish, or German.

Libraries that were government depository libraries in 1942 should have this in their collection.

Harvey, Cecil L. *Agriculture of the American Indian, a Select Bibliography*. Bibliographies and Literature of Agriculture No. 4. Washington, D.C.: United States Department of Agriculture; Science and Education Administration; Economics, Statistics, and Cooperative Service, 1979.

An updating of the Edwards and Rasmussen bibliography above, this list includes books, parts of books, articles in journals, reports, and a few children's books. Reproduced from typescript, it covers "two continents and about 7000 years" discussing native American crops, Indian technology, settlement patterns, economics, family organization, and ritual as they relate to agriculture. While the last few pages focus on agriculture on U.S. and Canadian reservations today, the "writings, for the most part, discuss research

---

*In this annotated bibliography each topic may have four components: monographs (listed alphabetically by author); followed by bibliographies (also listed alphabetically by author); Library of Congress subject headings; and journal titles.

Not all of the topics have all of these components. The subject headings are given so that more books on the same topic may be found in a library's card catalog.

on agriculture when native American cultures were strong and healthy. During this time, Indians developed as much as 60 percent of the crops used in today's diet. Important foods such as potatoes, chocolate, corn, squash, beans and turkeys are just a small part of their contribution. Their farms ranged from garden size to the size of plantations. (They) also had well developed pharmaceuticals from roots and herbs" (preface).

Subject heading: "Indians of North America – Agriculture."

### Alcohol

Mail, Patricia D., and David R. McDonald, comps. *Tulapai to Tokay: A Bibliography of Alcohol Use and Abuse Among Native Americans of North America.* New Haven: HRAF Press, 1980.

"With a Foreword and Literature Review by Joy H. Leland and Indexes by Sandra Norris" (title page).

"General consensus among a wide variety of observers, coupled with substantial medical, criminal justice, and behavioral science data support the contention that alcohol use and abuse is widespread among the native peoples of North America" (preface, p. xii).

In a comprehensive and depressing work Mail and McDonald provide an annotated bibliography of more than 969 journal articles, books, chapters in books, unpublished papers, conference reports, dissertations, government documents, and so on, concerning this topic. (There are another seventy-eight unannotated entries.)

The authors represent a "broad range of training, experience, ethnicity, and disciplinary perspective" (p. vii).

The bibliography itself is preceded by a forty-nine page review of the literature, discussing the association between Native American problem drinking and suicide, homicide, other crimes, the alcohol use by various subpopulations (youth, city dwellers), the treatment of problem drinkers, and the various explanations for the drinking behavior (physical, social deprivation, cultural, and so on).

Most of the entries refer to the United States but about 13 percent deal with the native peoples of Canada.

(Information is given for how to obtain the unpublished material.)

Subject headings: "Indians of North America – Alcohol use"; "Indians of North America – Liquor problem."

### Anthropology

Murdock, George P. and Timothy J. O'Leary. *Ethnographic*

*Bibliography of North America.* 5 vols. New Haven: Human Relations Area Files Press, 1975.

Providing 40,000 citations to literature on the native peoples of North America up to 1972, the major focus here is on ethnographic description followed by linguistics, archaeology, history, relations with the federal governments, education, medicine, human geography, urbanism and Pan-Indianism. The North American continent is covered down to the northern boundary of Mesoamerica.

There is neither author nor subject index. (A specific topic must be found by scanning the table of contents for likely headings.)

Volume I is General North America; Volume II, Arctic and Subarctic; Volume III, Far West and Pacific Coast; Volume IV, Eastern United States; and Volume V, Plains and Southwest.

This is a monumental work.

Subject headings: "Indians of North America." Books on a specific tribe will have that tribe's name as a subject heading (e.g., "Cayuga Indians"; "Delaware Indians"; "Peoria Indians"; "Potawatomi Indians"; "Seneca Indians"; "Shawnee Indians"; etc.).

## Archaeology

Jennings, Jesse D. *Prehistory of North America.* 2d ed. New York: McGraw-Hill, 1974.

In this introductory textbook to the archaeology of North America Jennings covers, among other topics, the dating techniques of archaeology (dendrochronology, radiocarbon, etc.); the theories of how man came to be in the New World; the early cultures (Llano, Folsom, Plano); the archaic stage (by region—Eastern Archaic, the Northeast, the Midlands, and so on); Mexico and the domestication of plants; the rise, climax, and decline of the Hopewell, the Mississippian, etc., cultures and of those of the Southwest such as the Hohokam, Mogollon, and more, on up to the Arctic.

Jennings's approach is culture-historical—how cultures differ one from another and how they evolved.

Many black-and-white illustrations—arrowheads and other stone artifacts, chronological tables, pottery specimens, outline maps, and so on—as appropriate for a textbook are included here.

In the preface to the first edition, reprinted in this second edition, Jennings says his intent is not to create an encyclopedic reference work but a book which is "not the last but the first word on the subject for many readers" (p. x).

In this he has succeeded.

Snow, Dean R. *The Archaeology of North America.* Photographs by Werner Forman. New York: Viking Press, 1976. (Published in England under the title *The American Indians: Their Archaeology and Prehistory.*)

"Through [archaeology] we have rediscovered the achievements of the Indians of North America, achievements which range across the whole spectrum of human culture. Their monuments were built of earth, wood, and grass more often than stone. Their arts were practiced in fiber, clay, wood, or flint. Their most precious materials were copper, mica, shell . . . obsidian . . . galena, none of which have much intrinsic value to European minds. Yet these, and others even more commonplace, were the media of prehistoric North American artisans. It is the quality of their achievements in these media, not the intrinsic values of the materials themselves, to which this volume is dedicated" (introduction, pp. 7–8).

Organized around the "'lifeways'" of America's early inhabitants and arranged by regional area – Eastern Woodlands, Great Plains, Desert West, Far West, Arctic and Subarctic – this smoothly written book with its many photographs (masks, gorgets, fertility charms, pottery, arrowheads, shields, baskets, blankets, and still-extant cliff dwellings) makes a fine introduction for the layperson to the early Americans whose ancestors came across the Bering Strait on a land bridge some 27,000 years ago.

There are maps and chronologies for each area, a short bibliography, no footnotes, and a minimum of technical jargon.

Snow, Dean R. *Native American Prehistory, a Critical Bibliography.* Newberry Library Center for the History of the American Indian Bibliographic Series. Bloomington: Indiana University Press, 1979.

"Native Americans have inhabited this continent since well before the end of the last great glaciation, probably about 27,000 years. Yet we have written records for fewer than the past 600 . . . . For all that time and space we must rely upon the work of archaeologists or give up ever knowing how the cultural diversity of historic native Americans came about" (p. vii).

Following the standard format of the Newberry bibliographic series (a bibliographic essay followed by a list of titles), Snow gives his thoughts on what are the best books on North American prehistory and the best introductory books on general archaeology.

He also treats, briefly, books on the Mesoamerican background of North America and on the "earliest" Americans, noting that books on this subject published before 1970 should be avoided as many of the sites mentioned in earlier sources have been discredited, more recently discovered sites do not appear at all, and interpretations are generally out of date (p. 19).

The bibliographic essay concludes by describing regional works on the Eastern Woodlands, the Great Plains, the Desert West, the Far West, and the Arctic and Subarctic.

On the list of 204 titles which follows the essay, the works suitable for secondary students are marked with a star.

Subject headings: "Indians of North America—Antiquities"; Excavations (Archaeology)—by place, for example, "Excavations (Archaeology)—Arizona." Specific sites will be entered under the name of the site (e.g., "Koster site, Ill.").

Journals:     *American Antiquity.* v. 1, 1935–
Society for American Archaeology
1703 New Hampshire Ave., N.W.
Washington, D.C. 20009

*Early Man.* v. 1, 1979–
Center for American Archaeology
1911 Ridge Ave.
Evanston, IL 60201

*North American Archaeologist.* v. 1, 1979–
Baywood Publishing Co., Inc.
120 Marine St., Post Office Box D
Farmingdale, NY 11735

## *Art*

Dockstader, Frederick J. *Indian Art in America; the Arts and Crafts of the North American Indian.* Greenwich, Conn.: New York Graphic Society, 1961.

In a large and beautiful book, Dockstader attempts "to gather together a general selection of some of the finest examples of North American Indian art, together with some specimens of everyday craftsmanship which possess unusual aesthetic qualities . . . the goal has been to include every important region, most of the numerically or artistically preeminent tribes, and all the major techniques employed by Indian artists" (p. 13).

The chapter "The Indian as an Artist" discusses ritual and religion as it affected Indian art; the various characteristics of Indian art; the regionalism into which it can be divided (Dockstader uses nine major geographical areas); techniques, style, tradition ("traditional" Navajo silverwork did not begin until 1853); the sexual division of artistic production (only a few tribes let women make articles for religious uses, but aboriginally most pottery, basketry, beadwork, costuming, etc. was done by women); the sources of Indian designs—sometimes dreams or visions, sometimes from trade, sometimes "bought" from another creator; and so on.

The 248 illustrations, some mounted and in color, are accompanied by commentaries as to tribe, provenance, etc.

Since its first appearance in 1961 this book has been republished in several editions. Its most recent reprinting was in 1974 by Promontory Press. In 1970 the Graphic Society reprinted it "with additions to the bibliography" but with the same pagination, and with a slightly different title, *Indian Art in North America, Arts and Crafts*.

Feest, Christian F. *Native Arts of North America*. New York: Oxford University Press, 1980.

In this volume, a part of The World of Art series, which gives a straightforward overview of North American art, Feest observes that "none of the native languages of North America seem to contain a word that can be regarded as synonymous with the Western concept of art, which is usually seen as something separable from the rest of daily life . . . . The question that has to be answered first of all is how objects not conceived as art by their makers have come to be valued as art by their latter-day admirers." Feest tries to answer this question with a brief history of the "encounter between Europe and the manufacturers of the New World" (p. 9), and then goes on to divide Indian-produced art into four kinds. Tribal art, he says, is that produced in the past and now for tribal members own use or for that of their fellows. It has functionality as an overriding criterion and is not made for its own sake but to satisfy material or spiritual needs. Ethnic art is that produced by tribal members for the use of other groups (primarily white Americans) and mostly as a source of income. Pan-Indian art is produced for the art market by Indians who regard themselves simply as artists and as not bound to the customs of their original tribe. This art is often shaped by white expectations about Indian style and uses nontraditional media. The last kind of Indian art is mainstream art produced by artists who happen to be Indian. This can be any kind of art and is not discussed in this book.

To describe these first three kinds of art, Feest arranges his book by techniques and styles and goes from prehistoric times to the present. Major divisions are painting and engraving; textiles; and sculpture. (Sculpture, for example, is further divided into stone sculpture; wood carving; ivory, bone, and horn sculpture; clay sculpture; and "other three-dimensional arts"—e.g., land art such as the Serpent Mound.)

Each section has its own bibliography, and there are nearly 200 illustrations, mostly in black and white, with a few in color.

Harding, Anne D., and Patricia Bolling. *Bibliography of Articles and Papers on North American Indian Art.* New York: Kraus Reprint, 1969.

Originally published in Washington, D.C., 1938, with Department of the Interior, Indian Arts and Crafts Board at head of title. (The Kraus reprint has the spine title *Bibliography on North American Indian Art.*)

Harding and Bolling list the articles concerning Indian arts and crafts from about 115 scholarly series and journals. Part I is the list arranged alphabetically by author. Parts II, III, and IV are various rearrangements of this list—by area, by specific technique and product, by tribe (under cultural area), and by craft. Crafts listed include basketry; bead and quillwork; birchbark; body painting and tattooing; bone, horn, and ivory; clothing; dyes and pigments; featherwork; games; hairwork; petroglyphs and pictographs; pottery; projectiles; shellwork; stone; tanning; weaving; etc.

Reproduced from typescript.

Karpel, Bernard, ed. *Arts in America, a Bibliography.* 4 vols. Washington, D.C.: Smithsonian Institution Press, 1979.

Section A of Volume I is "Art of the Native Americans."

Except for some classic works, Karpel does not duplicate titles listed in the Harding and Bolling work preceding. He lists significant titles published since that book appeared and attempts "to provide by appropriate classifications, section head-notes, and subject cross-references—a valid and more popular guide to the arts and crafts of the Native American" (introduction).

His unannotated list of 1,392 titles includes books, chapters in books, articles in journals, pamphlets, leaflets (some as short as two pages), catalogs of exhibitions, and serials. It is divided into twelve categories: bibliography; general works on the background of Indian and Eskimo culture; art in general; exhibition catalogs; serials; specific art subjects with cross-references to the tribal and regional categories; the Eskimo; the Northwest Coast; the Eastern Woodlands; the Plains; the Southwest; and the Far West. (Some Canadian material is included but the emphasis is on the United States.)

The "specific art subjects" section includes titles on architecture, basketwork, bead and quillwork, ceramics, costume, leatherwork, masks, metalwork, painting, contemporary painting, petroglyphs, sculpture, shellwork, stonework, and textiles.

The 1,392 titles cover sixty-nine two-column unnumbered pages.

For students, scholars, museum workers, and serious hobbyists, this is an essential work.

Subject headings: "Indians of North America – Art"; "Indians of North America – Costume and adornment"; "Indians of North America – Pictures, illustrations, etc."; "Indians of North America – Pictorial works"; "Indians of North America – Portraits"; "Indians of North America – Sculpture"; "Indians of North America – Silversmithing." (See also the subject headings under Crafts.)

Journal:     *American Indian Art Magazine.* v. 1, 1975–
             7333 E. Monterey Way #5
             Scottsdale, AZ 85251

### *Artifacts*

Brennan, Louis A. *Artifacts of Prehistoric America.*
Harrisburg, PA: Stackpole Books, 1975.

Drawing on thirty years' experience, Brennan put in "a single volume of manageable size the verbal and visual descriptions of the customary tools, equipment and material possessions of the Amerind – the American aborigine – and enough information about their manufacture, presumed use and cultural placement to make them comprehensible as archaeological data." Chapters cover artifact classification; the technology of chipped stone; pecked, ground and polished stone; rough stone artifacts; antler, bone, vegetal fiber and wood; artifacts of metal; and ceramics. Many black-and-white photographs accompanied by succinct paragraphs on how the object was made and on its use make this an excellent reference tool for preliminary identification of artifacts. Although there is no glossary as such, the index can be used to look up names and words in the jargon of the New World archaeologist ("Folsom," "Sandia," "birdstone," etc.).

Hothem, Lar. *North American Indian Artifacts*. 2d ed. A Collector's Identification and Value Guide. Florence, Ala. and New York: Crown Publishers, 1980.

The author calls baskets, blankets and rugs, jewelry, and pottery the "Big Four" of Amerind collectibles (p. 313), but there is much more here than the Big Four in this well-illustrated collectors's guide. Chapters cover arrowheads and other chipped artifacts (blades, drills, spades); antler, bone, and shell objects (spoons, awls, necklaces); axes; stone collectibles (such as discoidals, mortars and pestles); bannerstones, banded slate ornaments (e.g., birdstones); copper and hematite artifacts; pottery; trade era collectibles (axes, pipe-tomahawks, silver ornaments, beads); baskets; bead and quillwork; pipes; clothing and moccasins; wooden collectibles (cradleboards, masks, and such); dolls and toys; blankets and rugs; and jewelry. Many of the chapters conclude with suggested readings of from one to four titles.

For each specimen listed there are one or two lines describing it and a representative price, or price range, given. The prices are designated A (auction); C (collector); D (dealer), and G (gallery).

There is also a chapter titled "What are Amerind Collectibles Really Worth?" and sections giving addresses of businesses which handle American Indian material; and of auction houses, amateur archaeological organizations, the Indian Arts and Crafts Association (to which one can write for a directory of members), the Indian Arts and Crafts Board of the United States Department of the Interior, and so on.

The last few pages of the book are a glossary, with black-and-white sketches, of point and blade types.

While the many pictures in the body of the book are in black and white there is a thirty-two-page insert of stunning color photographs of blankets, pottery, beadwork, etc.

Useful for collectors, hobbyists, and craftsmen and fun for browsers as well.

Miles, Charles. *Indian and Eskimo Artifacts of North America*. New York: Bonanza Books, 1963.

This is a wonderful "pictorial catalog," as Frederick Dockstader called it in his foreword, of some 2,000 "human-altered objects" made and used by North American Indians and Eskimos.

The headings of the chapters are "Food"; "Homes and Housekeeping"; "Manufacturing"; "Pre-Columbian Clothing"; "Personal Adornment"; "Ceremony and Religion"; "Toys; Games and Sport"; "Smoking"; "Travel"; and "Combat." Each chapter is further subdivided as appropriate. Thus under "Food" are pictures of baskets and nets; digging tools; clubs, bolas, and rabbit sticks (curved sticks similar to boomerangs but nonreturning); spears, darts, and lances; and so on. Under "Homes" are pictures of fire-making apparatus including shredded-bark slow matches for carrying fire from place to place; under "Clothing" is footgear, hats and caps, and personal effects (such as an elkhorn louse crusher); under "Personal Adornment" there are beads, necklaces, head and limb adornment, and jewelry; under "Ceremony and Religion" are masks, birdstones, and charm stones; under "Smoking," a wonderous variety of pipes and tobacco accessories; and so on.

For many of the items the author does not give tribal identification, but this is a book for nonspecialists and the total effect, which comes from the introductions to the chapters, the few lines accompanying each picture, and the pictures of the objects themselves, is to show how the first Americans lived their ordinary lives.

There are a few color plates, but the illustrations are primarily small black-and-white photographs. Most of the specimens are from the author's own collection.

Subject headings: See the subject headings under Archaeology, Art, and Crafts.

Journal:      *Hobbies; the Magazine for Collectors.* v. 1, 1931–
              Lightner Publishing Corp.
              1006 S. Michigan Ave.
              Chicago, IL 60605

## *Authors, Indians*

Hirschfelder, Arlene, comp. *American Indian and Eskimo Authors, a Comprehensive Bibliography.* New York: Association on American Indian Affairs, 1973.

Lists "almost 400 titles written or narrated by nearly 300 Indian and Eskimo authors representing more than 100 tribes . . . ." There are all kinds of works here: folktales, autobiographies, poems, novels, ethnographies, and so on. The titles have one-or two-sentence annotations.

*Indian-Inuit Authors; an Annotated Bibliography. Auteurs Indiens et Inuit; Bibliographie Annotée.* Ottawa: Information Canada, 1974. 108 p.

As the title says, this is an annotated list of works by Canadian native authors (children as well as adults) published up to and including 1972. The parallel text in French and English covers, in the Indians and Metis section: anthologies; collected works; poetry and songs; articles; addresses; conferences, reports, studies, theses; language; and texts. (These last two categories have works on or in a native language.)

While the writings can be on any subject, the older ones tend to be autobiographies and legends, and the more recent ones are articles on educational problems or the contemporary political scene.

Lack of a subject or title index makes this a book which must be used primarily by browsing. Still, it is by browsing that one comes across such unexpected titles as Louis Jackson's *Our Caughnawagas in Egypt* (Montreal: Drysdale, 1885) about which the annotation says "The writer, a Mohawk, was the captain of the group of 52 Indians from Caughnawaga who took part in the expedition of North American Indian voyageurs sent in 1884 to help in the relief on Khartoum" (p. 7).

Littlefield, Daniel F., Jr., and James W. Parins. *A Bio-bibliography of Native American Writers,* 1772–1924. Native American Bibliography Series No. 2. Metuchen, N.J.: Scarecrow Press, 1981.

Here we have a list of 4,371 published letters, political essays and addresses, satirical works in various dialects, poetry, fiction, myths, legends, historical works, and reminiscences written in English by Native Americans. They "vary widely in form, technique and quality and [yet] provide valuable insights into the Native American's self-concept throughout the decades" (p. xiii).

Much of the writing reflects the trends of popular writing among non-Indians of the time, but in most some use of the writer's native background was made despite his or her degree of acculturation. A major theme of many was the "Indian problem"—how Indians cope in and with white society.

Writers listed include Charles A. Eastman, Gertrude Simmons Bonnin, John Oskison, Will Rogers, Rolla Lynn Riggs, Charles

Curtis, Robert Latham Owens, Francis La Flesche, Arthur C. Parker, John N. B. Hewitt, and William Jones.

Part II is a "Bibliography of Native American Writers Known Only by Pen Names," and Part III, "Biographical Notes" has from a sentence to a paragraph of information on every identified writer. There is also an index to writers by tribal affiliation and a subject index.

No Canadians are included.

Subject heading; "American literature – Indian authors. (See also the Literature section.)

Note: Data on Indian authorship for documents in the ERIC data base have been kept since mid-1979. Approximately 22 percent of the documents on Indian education entered in ERIC from mid-1979 to March 1980 were written by Indians. From April 1980 to February 1981 approximately 30 percent of the documents on Indian education were of Indian authorship. (American Indian Education Fact Sheet, October 1981, the ERIC Clearinghouse on Rural Education and Small Schools. New Mexico State University, Las Cruces, N.M.)

### Autobiography and Biography

Brumble, H. David, *An Annotated Bibliography of American Indian and Eskimo Autobiographies.* Lincoln: University of Nebraska Press, 1981.

"Many of those who look through this book will be surprised at the number of entries – over 500 autobiographical narratives, well over one hundred of which are book length. The earliest date back to the eighteenth century . . . . Here are mothers, fathers, warriors, G.I.'s, preachers, pilots, pitchers, authors, artists, shamans, doctors, hunters, Peyotists, Methodists, visionaries, spiritualists, politicians, and at least one cannibal" (p. 1).

The compiler has tried to include all printed versions of first-person narratives by North American Indians and Eskimos, even if only one page long. (He also includes a few titles which are wrongly, he says, listed elsewhere as American Indian autobiographies.)

Early pietistic tales of conversion, accounts of life in boarding schools, reminiscences of Indian wars, World War II memoirs, stories of prereservation life, narratives of hunting and trapping, books which in one volume combine tribal and mythic history with personal history or tell what it is like to grow up between two cultures – they're all here.

In the annotations, care is taken to determine the extent a collaborator or white questioner played in the actual composition of the work, and for some entries literary criticism of the book is noted. (Thus the entry for *Black Elk Speaks* cites the article *"Black Elk Speaks* and So Does John Neihardt," *Western American Literature* 6, No. 4 (Winter 1972): 231–42.)

The author provides a thoughtful introduction discussing the, at times, editorial distortion of American Indian autobiographies by anthropologists or other Indian enthusiasts, and some notes on autobiography in general.

Books likely to appeal to high-school students are starred, and if the book was in print in 1979, that is noted.

Dockstader, Frederick J. *Great North American Indians, Profiles in Life and Leadership.* New York: Van Nostrand Reinhold, 1977.

In *Great North American Indians,* Dockstader profiles 300 men and women who lived from the 1500s to the 1970s. Portraits of the biographees are included if it was possible, and there are also pictures of Indian artifacts which add to the eye-appeal of the book. Indian naming customs are discussed in the introduction which tells how hard it is to get accurate biographical information on Indians. Sometimes an Indian would simply supply a name at random just to get rid of the questioner; or translations could shift the meaning. Dockstader gives as one example the name of Wahbahse usually translated as "'Dawn of the Day" or 'He Causes Brightness,' suggesting a poetic reference to enlightenment or a bright beginning. But in his own words, the term came from "When I killed the enemy, he was pale, like the light of early morning'" (p. 4). One person could have several different names through a lifetime, hereditary names could be handed down from one generation to the next, making it hard to know which same-named person was involved, some names were public, some private, individuals could have both white and Indian names, and so on.

This is a well-designed, attractive book saved from the coffee table category by its extensive bibliography.

Edmunds, R. David, ed. *American Indian Leaders, Studies in Diversity.* Lincoln: University of Nebraska Press, 1980.

Here are biographies by twelve different writers of men who exercised "varieties of Indian political leadership within the realm of Indian-white relations" (p. xiv).

Some of the men portrayed, Satana (Kiowa) and Sitting Bull (Hunkpapa) resisted any compromise with the whites. Others, Old Briton (Miami) and Joseph Brant (Mohawk) allied themselves with the Europeans and some, the mixed-bloods – Alexander McGillivray (Creek); John Ross (Cherokee); Dennis Bushyhead (Cherokee); and Quanah Parker (Comanche) – used the tools acquired by their white education to benefit their tribes, and also to benefit themselves financially.

Other leaders portrayed are Red Bird (Winnebago), Washakie (Shoshone), Carlos Montezume (Yavapai), and Peter MacDonald (Navajo). MacDonald is the only living biographee.

All of the chapters have long bibliographies and black-and-white maps which place the scene of the action.

Josephy, Alvin M., Jr. *The Patriot Chiefs, A Chronicle of American Leadership*. New York: The Viking Press, 1961.

Another example of collective biography but written by a single author is Josephy's *Patriot Chiefs* which in colorful and moving chapters tells the stories of Hiawatha (Mohawk or Onondaga), King Philip (Wampanoag), Pope (Pueblo), Pontiac (Ottawa), Osceola (Tallassee), Black Hawk (Sauk), Crazy Horse (Sioux), and Chief Joseph (Nez Perce).

This popular book remains in print, more than twenty years after it was first published, as *Patriot Chiefs, a Chronicle of American Indian Resistance*, Penguin, 1969 (paperback).

Subject headings: "Indians of North America – Biography." (The subject heading for a book on an individual is that individual's name.)

### Bows and Arrows

Hamilton, T. M. *Native American Bows*. 2d ed. With an Appendix by Bill Holm on Making Horn Bows. Also Photos of Horn Bows from the Collection of Charles E. Grayson. Missouri Archaeological Society Special Publications No. 5. Columbia, Mo.: Missouri Archaeological Society, 1982.

"I am not an anthropologist, but an archer, and my interest is how the Indians built their bows and how well they shot" (p. xiv). So says the author in the foreword to this book which is the result of a labor of love extending over seventeen years.

To write his book Hamilton assembled and critiqued all the information on American Indian bows which he could find, working from the accounts of the early explorers, the paintings of the artists who visited the Indians, the reports of the anthropological experts (e.g., Saxton Pope), his own collection, and his own experience as archer and bowyer (one who makes bows).

Headings in the table of contents are: Bow Types and Classifications; The Dart and the Arrow; The Self-Bow; The Reinforced Bow; The Eskimo Bow and the Asiatic Composite; The American Composite; The Plains Bow in Action; On Making Horn Bows by Bill Holm; Horn Bows in the Grayson Collection; Actual Bow Performances; Tabulation of Bow Performances; Description of Ten Horn Bows in the U.S. National Museum.

The monograph is illustrated with black-and-white drawings and photographs; there is a glossary, a bibliography, and an index.

Laubin, Reginald, and Gladys Laubin. *American Indian Archery*. Norman: University of Oklahoma Press, 1980.

The Laubins begin their book with a history of archery which compares the bows of various eras and geographic regions (e.g., English longbows versus Indian bows) and cites the writings and pictures of the early white observers of Indian archery. Following chapters cover bow making and sinewed bows, horn bows, and strings. (Here, Laubin himself makes a concession to modern times and uses dacron, but he tells how to make sinew strings, observing that they are "highly affected by weather. When it rained the Indians called off a fight)" (p. 107). Also covered are quivers, and shooting (the ways the Indians hunted buffalo and deer, the tricks of the "show" Indians), the various finger positions for releasing arrows, and the like. Shorter chapters cover medicine bows (bows not used as weapons but thought to have special powers), blowguns used by the Cherokees, and there are even a few paragraphs on the bows used by some South American Indians to shoot stones or clay balls.

Differing customs of each tribe as to decoration and materials used for construction are also described.

There is enough information here for the perservering craftsman to make his or her own bow in the Indian manner (if he or she has the time and realizes that working with sinew and bone can be a hot, smelly business.) The building of many bows is described in detail, and there are clear, black-and-white drawings of bow cross-sections, bows of wood and of horn, and types of nocks. There are also color photographs of quivers and of beautifully decorated bows from all perspectives, strung and unstrung, so that one may see the quite different curvature.

Laubin includes tales of his own shooting experiences and those of the elderly Indian friends with whom he consulted, and the whole is like a long, friendly conversation with a man who is doing something he enjoys.

Subject headings: "Bow and arrow"; "Indians of North America – Arms and armor."

## Canada

*Indian Conditions: a Survey.* Ottawa: Minister, Indian and Northern Affairs, 1980. Catalogue No. R32-45/1980E.

"Cette Publication peut aussi être obtenue en français."

In 1961 there were 180,000 Indians in Canada. In 1979 there were 300,000 in 573 bands. They include ten different language groups and fifty-eight dialects. Some 30 percent live outside Indian reserves (compared to less than 16 percent in 1966). There are 2,242 separate parcels of reserve land with a total of 10,021 square miles. The average band size has grown from 350 to 525 in 1979. (The smallest band was New Westminister with two members. The largest was Six Nations of the Grand River with 9,950.) About 65 percent live in rural communities (compared with 25 percent of the national population). The Indian population has been growing faster than the non-Indian since the 1950s. Life expectancy is ten years less than the national population. Violent deaths are three times national levels. Between fifty percent and 70 percent receive social assistance. One in three families lives in crowded conditions . . . (p. 3).

Graphs, charts, and tables with brief written commentary summarize the statistical information available on Canadian Indians generally comparing conditions as they were in the 1950s and 1960s to those in the late 1970s. Chapter headings include: "Social Conditions," "Economic Conditions," "Political Conditions," "Government Programs," "Off-Reserve," and "Reference Reading."

"The report is necessarily from a governmental point of view and is limited to what can be described by the available data" (p. 1).

First rate for background information.

Jenness, Diamond. *The Indians of Canada.* 7th ed. Toronto: University of Toronto in association with the National Museum of Man, National Museum of Canada and Publishing Centre, Supply and Services, Ottawa, Canada. 1977.

Originally published in 1932 as Bulletin 65, Anthropological Series No. 15 of the National Museum of Canada, Part One of this

7th edition covers languages; economic conditions; food resources; hunting and fishing; dress and adornment; dwellings; travel, transportation, trade, and commerce; social and political organization; social life; religion; folklore and traditions; theories as to the origin of Indians; and "interaction of Indians and whites." Part Two describes individual tribes by regional area: Eastern Woodlands; Plains, Pacific Coast; Cordillera; Mackenzie and Yukon River Basins; and Eskimos.

Quotes from the writings of the early explorers give lots of solid detail here on how Indians actually lived, the clothes they wore and the food they ate. The book is illustrated with black-and-white photographs and written in a style that contemporary readers may find both stilted and patronizing, nevertheless, it remains the best overall survey of how Canadian Indians lived at the time of white contact.

Abler, Thomas S., and Sally M. Weaver, *A Canadian Indian Bibliography 1960-1970*. Includes Case Law Digest prepared by Douglas E. Sanders. Toronto: University of Toronto Press, 1974.

This jumbo-sized bibliography on Canadian Indians and Metis is in three parts. The first part is a list of 1,417 items of "scholarly interest" which were published between 1960 and 1970. These items are grouped by such subjects as: general and comparative studies; legislation (bills and acts); Indian administration and government policy; history; demography; material culture; education; economics; social organizations; politics and law; medicine; religion; oral tradition and folklore; music and dance; and urban. The second part of the book is the case law digest on Canadian Indian legal questions. It consists of 241 items and covers a much longer period — 1867 to 1972. The third part consists of 1,379 items (also published between 1960 and 1970) arranged first by region (Sub-Arctic, Northwest Coast, Plateau, Plains, and Eastern Woodlands) and within region by tribe. (A last section is devoted to the Metis.)

The items in the first and third parts are books, journal articles, theses, and unpublished reports and papers; the items in the second part are legal decisions. All of the citations have annotations which vary in length from one or two sentences to a paragraph.

There is a subject index but no author index.

Canada. Indian and Eskimo Affairs Program. Education and Cultural Support Branch. *About Indians, a Listing of Books*. 4th ed. Ottawa: Minister of Indian and Northern Affairs, 1977.

An excellent list of books about Indians for all ages and interests. The 1,452 titles annotated here are arranged according to levels: kindergarten to grade 3; grade 3 to grade 6; and grade 6 "to beyond." The reviews were written by Canadian Indian university students who summarize the content and style of each book and who may make positive, or negative, remarks about the book from an Indian point of view.

The books are mainly about North American Indians, but there are a few about South America. Books by Canadian authors or having specific Canadian interest are marked with a maple leaf and there is a section of books written in the French language.

It is illustrated with a few stunning color photographs of contemporary Indian art.

There are author, title, and subject indexes.

The Canadian government documents catalogue number for this book is R32–30/1977. It is also in the Educational Resources Information Center microfiche collection. The ERIC number is ED157644.

Surtees, Robert J. *Canadian Indian Policy, a Critical Bibliography.* Bloomington: Indiana University Press, 1982.

The fifty-nine-page bibliographical essay in this title of the Newberry Library Center for the History of the American Indian Bibliographical Series gives a fine, clear introduction to Canadian Indian-white relationships from the time of the first French contact up to and beyond the dramatic White Paper (*Statement of the Government of Canada on Indian Policy*) of 1969 which recommended the abolition of the Indian department and repeal of the Indian Act and which prompted a new interest in Indian affairs generally.

Surtees divides the essay into three time periods: the French, 1608–1763; the British, 1763–1867; and the Canadian, 1867–1980; and covers writings on missionaries, the fur trade, reserves, imperialism, wars, politics, legal problems, Indian history and historiography and so on.

In the unannotated list of 293 books, journal articles, and government documents concluding the book, those titles suitable for secondary school students are so marked. Identified also are eleven works "for the beginner," and another thirteen works "for a basic library collection."

Whiteside, Don (sin a paw). *Aboriginal People: a Selected Bibliography Concerning Canada's First People.* Ottawa: National Indian Brotherhood, 1973.

In his introduction the compiler identifies several problems with the usual "'professional bibliography'" compiled on "Aboriginal People." Many of the studies and reports on aboriginal people are mimeographed, tend to have a limited circulation and then become lost; analytical material about aboriginal relations in Canada and articles on the philosophy and acts of resistance of aboriginal people appear in newspapers (usually omitted from professional bibliographies); and material about aboriginal people in other countries is not included in professionally-compiled bibliographies.

Accordingly, "This bibliography while it contains a fair sampling of the major published works, emphasizes unpublished speeches, reports, and proceedings of various conferences as well as salient newspaper articles . . . [it] also emphasizes the works of Aboriginal People . . . and includes a section on Aboriginals in other than North American countries" (p. i).

Sample headings from the table of contents are: "History of Native Peoples . . . ;" "Values, Traditions, Tales, Crafts, Biographies"; "Religious Beliefs . . . ;" "Aboriginal Rights and Treaties"; "The Indian Acts"; "Discussion of Indian Administration"; "Aboriginal Associations and Conferences"; "Resistance"; "Community Development;" "Formal Education;" etc.

There are author and subject indexes and for a reproduction fee most of the unpublished material is available from the National Indian Brotherhood Library, Ottawa.

Lots of good primary source material on the Canadian Indian scene is cited here.

Subject heading: "Indians of North America—Canada." (If the book is on Indians of one province, the subject heading will be, for example, "Indians of North America—Alberta".)

Journals:   *Native People.* v. 1, 1969–
            Alberta Native Communications Society
            9311 60th Ave.
            Edmonton, Atla. T6E OC2

            *North/Nord.* v. 1, 1954–
            Publishing Centre, Supply & Services Canada
            Ottawa, Ont. K1A OS9

## *Captivities*

Levernier, James, and Hennig Cohen. *The Indians and Their Captives.* Contributions in American Studies, Number 31. Westport, Conn.: Greenwood Press, 1977.

"When Rip Van Winkle failed to return from a hunting trip into the Catskills, it was assumed that he had been 'carried away by the Indians.' The assumption was fairly safe. During the French and Indian Wars, which ended about the time Rip disappeared, possibly as many as two thousand captives were carried to Canada by the Indians as war prisoners. Countless others were adopted into Indian tribes and lost forever to white society. The Indian captivity was a massive historic reality. It helped to shape the national character, it provided substance for the artistic imagination, it defined basic issues in white culture, and it was made to serve a variety of purposes, not all of which were noble" (introduction, p. xiii).

This collection of excerpts from captivity narratives edited and compiled by Levernier and Cohen is divided into five sections: the "Discovery of the Indian"; "Trials of the Spirit" (the Jesuits, Puritans, and Quakers interpreted their captivities in a religious framework); the "Land Imperative" (propaganda for the removal of any obstacle); "Behind the Frontier" (tales told in the settled regions); and "Beyond the Frontier" (the captivity theme as used in plays, poems, fictions, and art work).

The editors note that there are about 2,000 captivity narratives, including variant editions, based on the experiences of more than 500 captives from the early sixteenth century to the 1870s. While the focus of this collection is on the narrative as a literary form, there is much to interest an ethnologist or social historian, and a bibliographical note at the end of the work lists other titles on Indian captivities.

Vaughan, Alden T. *Narratives of North American Indian Captivity.* Garland Reference Library of the Humanities, v. 370. New York: Garland Publishing Co., 1983.

Vaughan's bibliography is in three sections: "Narratives of Indian Captivities" (with frequency of subsequent editions listed and cross-references to the subject of the narrative if that person is not also the author); "Modern Studies of Narratives and Captivities" (e.g., critical reviews); and "Guides to Indian Ethnohistory."

There are 411 items in the bibliography which is preceded by a forty-page introduction by Wilcomb Washburn.

Subject heading: "Indians of North America – Captivities."

### Cooking

Kavasch, Barrie. *Native Harvests, Recipes and Botanicals of the American Indian.* New York: Random House, 1979.

"Native American cuisine is a continental cooking entirely our own. The basis of what has become most classic is uniquely American Indian: barbeques and clambakes, steamed lobsters and stuffed oysters, clam and corn chowders and gumbos, multitudes of cranberry creations, Boston baked beans, Brunswick stew, mincemeat pie and spoonbread, plus the infinite variety of cornbreads and puddings and dumpling . . . " (introduction, p. xvii).

This attractive book with its trim drawings of plants is part botanical guide and part cookbook with medical hints scattered throughout.

Chapter headings: "Natural Seasonings" (nuts, seeds, berries, etc., including how to make nut milk); "Native Soups" (Jerusalem artichoke, corn soup); "Native Vegetables" (Jerusalem artichoke, steamed young milkweed pods, caramelized arrowhead tubers); "Native Ferns, Lichens, Mosses" (Iceland Moss Jelly); "Wild Mushrooms" (directions for identifying, gathering, and preparing); "Wild Meats" (how to handle, including a recipe for raccoon pie); "Saltwater and Freshwater Harvests" (fish and shellfish); "Natural Breads" (elder-blossom fritters, Chippewa bannock, Navajo fry bread, cattail pollen cakes, and more); "Wilderness Beverages" (chicory, coltsfoot, birch drinks, linden tea — "excellent for colds" — "Wild Medicines and Cosmetics"; "Wild Smoking Mixtures"; "Natural Chewing Gum"; and, a very brief chapter on "Poisonous Wild Plants."

Many of the recipes here are similar to those that can be found in other cookbooks, especially those of the cooking-from-the-wild sort; but this book is stronger in botanical information and also gives some background information on Indian plant and animal usage.

There is a glossary, bibliography, botanical index and general index.

Kavena, Juanita Tiger. *Hopi Cookery*. Tucson: University of Arizona Press, 1980.

The recipes in this book are not derived from library research. They are the regular or ceremonial foods of the Hopi women quoted here (or at least those of their mothers).

In this warm and charming book the author, a home economist of Creek descent who married into the Hopi tribe, gives more than 100 recipes for foods based on crops grown on the Hopi reservation. The chapters are: "Beans," "Corn," "Wheat," Chilies," "Meat," "Native Greens and Fruits," "Gourds," "Beverages," "Between Meals," and "Special Information." Corn, which comes in white, yellow, red, blue, and speckled varieties, is the "focal point of Hopi culture and religion" (p. 13), and merits the longest chapter, as Hopi women regularly make more than thirty different corn dishes. Recipes for many of them are given here, including one for "piki" the tissue-thin cornbread baked on smooth piki stones which are handed down from mother to daughter as family heirlooms. There are also recipes for Hopi finger bread made from blue corn-meal, directions for making spoons from corn husks, and much more. The meat chapter includes baked prairie dog; jerky; venison, antelope, or elk swiss steak; pan-fried lamb; and so on. The native greens and fruit chapter covers boiled yucca fruit, dried salt greens, culinary ashes, etc. (Culinary ashes are made by burning certain bushes or trees. Creeks and Seminoles use hickory, and Navajos use juniper branches. The Hopis like the four-winged saltbush which adds high mineral content to the food, increasing the nutritional value, and also, when added to cornmeal, makes the distinctive blue-green color which has religious significance for the Hopis.)

The "between meals" chapter covers snacks such as parched beans (cooked in a cast iron pot in fine, clean sand) and more, and the special information chapter lists foods suitable for times of fasting and gives the mineral content of selected Hopi foods.

For most of the foods given here the Hopi name is given, and notes as to customary usage – a breakfast dish, a wedding food, prepared by women working together – are added.

In addition to being a source of authentic Hopi recipes, this book would be suitable for supplementary reading in a women's studies course as it provides insights into a Hopi woman's everyday life.

Keegan, Marcia *Pueblo & Navajo Cookery*. Dobbs Ferry, New York: Earth Books, a Division of Morgan & Morgan, 1977.

This collection of about eight-five recipes was put together by a photographer who was also once a food editor. She has illustrated her book with glorious color photographs of Pueblo and Navajo country and of the local Indians dancing, cultivating the field, scattering cornmeal as a prayer at sunrise, dipping water at the water hole, or using the "horno" (abode outdoor oven). There are also, of course, photographs of food. Interspersed in the book are chants and prayers and quotes from Navajo and Pueblo men and women on how it was when they were children; the customs associated with grinding corn, the men singing and the women grinding to the rhythm of the songs for three or four hours; the dancing and fasting that preceded hunting and the sharing of the animal after a successful hunt; and so on.

The recipes are divided into soups and appetizers (Zuni corn soup, corn salad, guacamole); vegetable dishes (cracked chicos, corn and pumpkin stew); meat dishes (juniper lamb stew, feast-day pork roast); breads and desserts (Navajo kneeldown bread, frying pan corn bread, pinon cookies, fry bread pudding) and so on.

Kimball, Yeffe, and Jean Anderson. *The Art of American Indian Cooking*. Garden City, N.Y.: Doubleday, 1965.
  The 200 recipes here are suitable for contemporary kitchens and are divided into sections by region: The Gardeners of the Southwest, the Fishermen of the Pacific Northwest, the Wandering Hunters of the Plains, the Planters of the South, and the Woodsmen of the East. Each of these fancifully-titled sections includes soups, salads, main dishes, vegetables, breads, and desserts and is preceded by a lively introduction with brief bits of information on the history and environment of the area, the crops which grew there, the animals and fish available, and the etiquette and religious ceremonies associated with food. Frequently, there is also some early white visitor's mouth-watering description of a repast the Indians put before him. The artist George Catlin visiting the Mandan wrote of " . . . a fine brace of buffalo ribs, delightfully roasted; and . . . a kind of paste or pudding made of the flour of the *'pomme blanche'* as the French call it, a delicious turnip of the prairie, finely flavored with the buffalo berries which are collected in great quantities . . . " (p. 88). The naturalist William Bartram who visited the Seminole described red snapper steamed with fresh oranges, with whole oranges marinated in honey for several days, served as dessert (p. 127).
  Sample recipes: pinion cakes, grilled salmon steaks with juniper berries, leather britches beans, yellow squash blossoms, sunflower seed cakes, corn pone, wild rice johnnycakes, venison mincemeat, Iroquois [fish] soup, and so on.
  Subject headings: "Cookery, Indian"; "Indians of North America— Food."

## *Crafts*

Schneider, Richard C. *Crafts of the North American Indian: a Craftsman's Manual*. Cincinnati: Van Nostrand Reinhold, 1972.
  Written in a conversational style with historical background information thrown in (when glass beads were introduced, how they were made, etc.), the directions here are carefully detailed from start to finish. (The section on stone flaking starts, "Get a

supply of Band Aids.") The chapters cover tools, how to make moccasins, mittens, drums, beadwork, bark (from small containers to a brich bark canoe, starting with selection of the tree in the forest), basketry, ceramics, and fiber (corn husk dolls).

Illustrated with black-and-white drawings by the author, each chapter has a short reading list citing the scholarly source of information of each craft.

By a non-Indian artist and teacher who has "learned these crafts through a combination of book-study, observation, examination, conversation and actual experimentation" (p. v).

Subject headings: "Indians of North America – Industries"; "Indians of North America – Basket-Making"; "Indians of North America – Pottery"; "Indians of North America – Wood-carving"; "Indians of North America – Implements." (See also the subject headings under "Art".) "Indian craft" is the subject heading for works giving instruction and examples for duplicating Indian crafts.

### *Dance*

Laubin, Reginald and Gladys Laubin. *Indian Dances of North America, Their Importance to Indian Life.* Norman: University of Oklahoma Press, 1977.

Written by two non-Indians who have devoted their lives to Indian study (they also wrote *The Indian Tipi: Its History, Construction, and Use*), this book tries to cover all North American Indian dance. It succeeds best in describing fully the dances of the Northern Plains Indians, the Dakotas, Crows, and Tetons, with dances of other regions receiving less attention.

Dances described include various versions of the War Dance; Victory and Scalp Dance; the Green Corn Dance; Calumet and Eagle Dances; the Sun Dance; and so on. Much attention is paid to the proper costumes, and appearance (bustles, deer-hair roaches, body and facial painting), and information on singing and musical instruments as well as on customs and beliefs of the various tribes concerning dance is given.

The book is illustrated with paintings of dances by the famous white artists who visited Indians in the 1800s – George Catlin, Carl Bodmer, Paul Kane; drawings of dance accessories; photographs of Indians dancing; and perhaps too many photographs of the Laubins themselves in Indian costumes.

The extensive bibliography is primarily of the early explorers' writings and of the pre-1950 anthropological literature (despite the

1977 publication date). Still, the whole is informative and entertaining and reflects the Laubins lifetime of learning from the Indian elders; studying, performing, and caring about Indian dancing.

Subject headings: "Indians of North America—Dances"; "Indians of North America—Music."

### Education

Fuchs, Estelle, and Robert J. Havinghurst. *To Live on this Earth, American Indian Education.* Garden City N.Y.: Doubleday, 1972.

"With minor exceptions the history of Indian education had been primarily the transmission of white American education, little altered, to the Indian child as a one-way process. The institution of the school is one that was imposed by and controlled by the non-Indian society, its pedagogy and curriculum little changed for the Indian children, its goals primarily aimed at removing the child from his aboriginal culture and assimilating him into the dominant white culture. Whether coercive or persuasive, this assimilationist goal of schooling has been minimally effective with Indian children, as indicated by their record of absenteeism, retardation, and high dropout rates" (p. 19).

This book is based on the government-funded National Study of American Indian Education which resulted in more than fifty technical papers and studied in depth approximately forty different schools in twenty-six communities from Alaska to North Carolina to the American Southwest. The schools studied included the four major kinds attended by Indians: public, BIA day schools, BIA boarding schools, and mission schools. The report discusses (among many other topics) the mental ability of Indian children; their curriculum; their teachers; their education in general as seen by themselves, their parents, and their community leaders; the deficiencies of Indian education; and the need for Indian parent participation in the education of Indian children.

Small maps locate the community or reservation under discussion, and tables and charts give scores on aptitude tests, and such, as well as statistics on school-age population of Indian children, percentage in school, etc.

While this is a scholarly study, the descriptions of each school and community are clearly written, and direct quotations, from observers, teachers, and parents, give the picture of each situation—the repression of the boarding schools, the problems that go with bureaucracy and teacher mobility (books arriving long after the teacher requesting them has gone), and the standard high-school problems of dropouts and discipline complicated by the differences in the backgrounds of the (usually) white teachers and the Indian students.

Final sections of the book are two appendixes. The first is "Overview of the National Study of American Indian Education"; the second is "Summary and Critique of Research Methods for Study of Indian Education."

Szasz, Margaret Connell. *Education and the American Indian. The Road to Self Determination.* 2d ed. Albuquerque: University of New Mexico Press, 1977.

This is an absorbing picture of how the federal Indian policy, shifting from goals of assimilation, to termination, to self-determination (i.e., Indian control), affected the course of Indian education.

The book covers the period from 1928, when the famous Meriam report appeared, to the early 1970s and focuses on the Bureau of Indian Affairs role in the education of Indian children whether they were in boarding schools, Indian community day schools or in the local public schools (as happened for some after the Johnson-O'Malley Act of 1934 was passed to help the states, financially, in the education of Indian children). In the final chapters the author discusses school controlled by the Indians themselves – a phenomenon which began in the late 1960s.

The book is based on published material, archival sources, and interviews with some of those who were on the scene. Examined especially are the ideas and actions of the movers and thinkers of the New Deal era in Indian education: W. Carson Ryan, Director of Education for the BIA from 1930 to 1935; the "'spellbinding'" Willard Walcott Beatty, director from 1936 to 1952; and in the post–World War II period, Hildegard Thompson, director from 1952 to 1965. Ryan and Beatty tried to apply the benefits they saw in the Progressive Education movement to the teaching of Indian children. (To this end they promoted summer schools for the teachers.) They wanted, at least in the early years, to change the standard approach of teaching Indian children by the same methods and curricula that were used for middle-class white children to one that reflected and helped preserve the values of the children's Indian heritage. They also believed in practical vocational training for rural living. Thompson wanted to prepare Indian youths for an urban technological society.

They all had their problems.

There are black-and-white photographs of the chief actors in the drama: John Collier, Commissioner of Indian Affairs, 1933–1945; Ryan, Beatty, and Thompson, as well as photographs of Indian school pupil activities.

Notes and a bibliography conclude the work.

Thompson, Thomas, ed. *The Schooling of Native America.* Washington, D.C.: American Association of Colleges for Teacher Education in collaboration with the Teacher Corps, United States Office of Education. 1978.

These ten essays, all by Native Americans involved in Indian education, are the outgrowth of the Native American Teacher Corps Conferences of 1973. They speak of the cultural differences between whites and Indians and to the agony Indian children face in schools modeled on white patterns.

The preface sketches Indian education from how it was before the white man came, through the Jesuits who arrived in 1611, the Protestant mission schools up to the 1860s, the later assimilationist schools of the federal government, and on, up to the establishment of the experimental Rough Rock Demonstration School among the Navajos in 1966.

The essays themselves discuss multicultural teacher education at Rough Rock; interracial politics at an Indian-white experimental school; why Indian college students drop out; Indian Head Start programs; Native American studies at the university level and how they relate to Indian students; an "ideal" school system for Indians; how Indians can get control of their own schools; the kind of preparation teachers of Indian children should have; and more.

There are four appendixes. They give the important dates in Indian education from 1568 to 1975; list Indian education organizations; identify American Indian community colleges; and list the treaties dealing with Indian education.

(One date given in the first appendix is in error. Moor's Charity School, which was founded to educate Indian and white youths and later became Dartmouth College, was started in the 1700s, not 1617 as the chronology states.)

The book is attractively designed and is illustrated with old-time photographs of Indian school children at the activities of days gone by—solemn boys posing in their heavy uniforms, girls standing around a Maypole, etc.

There are also portraits of some of the contributors.
Subject headings: "Indians of North America – Education";
"Indians of North America – Canada – Education."

Journals:   *Canadian Journal of Native Education*, v. 1, 1973–
Intercultural Education Program
Dept. of Educational Foundations
Faculty of Education
University of Alberta
Edmonton, Alta. T6G 2G5

*Journal of American Indian Education,* v. 1, 1961–
Bureau of Educational Research and
Services of the College of Education
Arizona State University
Tempe, AZ 85281

*Folklore*

Ullom, Judith C., comp. *Folklore of the North American Indians,
an Annotated Bibliography.* Washington, D.C.: Library of Congress, 1969.

In her entry "North American Indian Folklore" in the *Standard Dictionary of Folklore, Mythology and Legend* (New York, 1950) 2: 798–802) Erminie Vogelin says "Prose narratives, songs, chants, formulae, speeches, prayers, puns, proverbs, and riddles are the chief form of oral expression found among North American native peoples. The first five forms are common to all North American groups; the last three occur less frequently, and only among a restricted number of tribes" (p. 798).

The Ullom bibliography here annotates 152 collections of these "prose narratives" (tales) from all over the North American continent. They are arranged by "Eleven culture areas including the Eskimo [as] outlined on a map reproduced from folklorist Stith Thompson's *Tales of the North American Indian*" (p. v).

The culture areas are Eskimo, Mackenzie, Plateau, North Pacific, California, Plains, Central Woodland, Northeast Woodland, Iroquois, Southeast and Southwest. Each section has a short introduction followed by source books, then by children's books. In general, these source materials are the publications of anthropologists and ethnologists who worked for museums or universities in the late nineteenth and early twentieth century, and the children's editions are the tales in these scholarly monographs retold for children. Less frequently, the children's editions are based on stories still told by the old people to children on the Indian reservations.

The annotations are long and thorough, and there are black-and-white illustrations.

Subject headings: "Folklore, Indian"; "Indians of North America—Legends." (See also Haywood, Charles, *A Bibliography of North American Folklore and Folksong*, in the Music section.)

### Games

Baldwin, Gordon C. *Games of the American Indian*. New York: W. W. Norton, 1969.

Written for young people, this book covers tops; dolls; whistles and other noisemakers (such as bull-roarers, which are made of a thin piece of wood tied to a string which, when whirled rapidly around the head, make a loud whizzing noise); children's games similar to tag, crack-the-whip, and blindman's buff; and contests of who-can-hold-your-breath-the-longest, which are played by several tribes.

The author also describes various kinds of running and jumping contests; kicking balls or sticks while running footraces at the same time; mock warfare (throwing mudballs at the other side with throwing sticks); toys, tiny pottery pots, and little clay animals; many versions of guessing games such as the hand game in which a small object is hidden in the hand, the other side guesses which hand, and the game ends when the tally sticks used to keep score are all in the possession of one side; stick games played by guessing which of two piles of a set of small sticks—the set always consisting of an uneven number—has the odd number; dice games; skill games such as throwing a pole at a rolling hoop; chunky, played with a stone disk five or six inches in diameter and two slender poles, the object being to slide the pole down the prepared alley and have it stop where the stone stopped rolling; snow-snakes (sending a wooden pole down an iced groove in the snow); lacrosse; bow-and-arrow target games; double ball (in most tribes a woman's game played with two balls tied together with a cord and thrown with sticks from one player to another to a goal at the end of the field); and finally, string figures, which can be very simple or very complicated.

Many black-and-white photographs or drawings of the toys or gaming objects are shown: Chippewa dolls made of cattails, or of pine needles; cane tubes used in the hidden ball game of the Pimas;

the corn-husk ring and feathered corncob darts used by the Hopi in the hoop and pole game. All of these and more contribute to making this book a fine introduction to the fun Indian children and adults had.

There is a bibliography and index.

Culin, Stewart. *Games of the North American Indians*. New York: Dover Publications, 1975.

(An unabridged republication of "Games of the North American Indians," from the *Twenty-Fourth Annual Report of the Bureau of American Ethnology to the Smithsonian Institution, 1902–1903*, originally published by the Government Printing Office in 1907.)

The games of the American Indians are divided into two general classes: games of chance and games of dexterity. (There are no games of calculation such as chess.) The games of chance fall into two categories: games in which dice-like implements are thrown to determine a number or numbers with the count being kept by sticks, pebbles, or an abacus, counting board or circuit; and games in which one or more players guess in which of two or more places an odd or particularly marked lot is hidden, success or failure resulting in the gain or loss of counters. The games of dexterity are: archery in its various forms; sliding javelins or darts along hard ground or ice; shooting at moving targets such as a netted wheel or ring; ball in several highly specialized forms; and racing games which also involve ball play. There is also a game similar to the European cup-and-ball. Children have amusements such as top-spinning and mimic fights, but many of these games described here are played only by the adults and usually at fixed seasons or at certain festivals and rites. Gambling or betting accompanies nearly all of the games.

Written in the stately prose of the late nineteenth century, this is a one-volume encyclopedia of the games which were played with implements by the American Indians. (Games such as tag are excluded.)

Explorers, ethnographers, military men, missionaries, doctors who lived and visited with the Indians, and the Indians themselves, are quoted on the games – how and when they were played, the legends associated with them, what the equipment was made with (varying kinds of wood, bone, and seeds were used for the sticks and dice; wood galls, stones, or leather stuffed with moss or deer hair for the balls, and so on.

The book has over one thousand illustrations, mostly drawings, a few photographs, and in the game descriptions it provides an amazing amount of incidental linguistic and ethnographic detail.

Subject heading: "Indians of North America—Games."

## Genealogy

Kirkham, E. Kay. *Our Native Americans and Their Records of Genealogical Value.* Logan, Utah: Everton Publisher, 1980.

"Finding your Indian ancestors is not the same as tracing white ancestry. An Indian name does not [always] indicate whether the person is a male or a female. An Indian usually had more than one name in his or her lifetime . . . . The spelling of Indian names is a big problem in the records . . . . When an Indian was not able to write his or her own name someone else did it for them . . . and might make a mistake in writing it down . . . the relationships that are given in the records change between different tribes of Indians. The meanings of such words as "brother," "uncle," etc. are not always the same . . . " (p. 1).

Written by a volunteer worker and former employee of the Genealogical Society of Utah, here is a valiant effort to provide a guidebook for Native Americans who want to trace their ancestry, whatever their CDIB (certification of degree of Indian blood).

Allotment records, annuity rolls, enrollment records, heirship records, census records, etc., are listed and described. Chapter IX, for example, is a listing of Indian records by tribe, state, and reservation with titles of books with genealogical information also included, and Chapter X describes the information available on the American Indian census rolls, 1885–1940, at the National Archives and gives the tribe/band index to the rolls.

(The sources cited are primarily government records although the author notes that many records are in the custody of tribal councils, various religious denominations, museums, and historical societies.)

Subjects heading: "Indians of North America—Genealogy.

## Health and Medicine

*Health Problems of U.S. and North American Indian Populations.* Papers by David Rabin, Bascom Anthony, Saul Harrison et al. New York: MSS Information Corporation, 1972. 287 p.

This volume is a collection of twenty-two journals articles reproduced exactly as they appeared in various journals. They concern diabetes, trachoma, measles vaccine, and deafness, etc., among

Indians. There is also an article "Anthropological and Physiological Observations on Tarahumara Endurance Runners."

In 1974 this publisher published four other volumes made up of articles reprinted from journals. They were: *Diagnosis and Treatment of Prevalent Diseases of North American Indian Populations: 1* (Papers by Melvin Lee and others); *Diagnosis and Treatment of Prevalent Diseases of North American Indian Populations: II* (Papers by Max J. Miller and others); *Community Health and Mental Health Care Delivery for North American Indians* (Papers by E. Fuller Torrey and others); and *Anthropological Studies Related to Health Problems of North American Indians* (Papers by Robert S. Corruccini and others).

Vogel, Vergil J. *American Indian Medicine.* Norman: University of Oklahoma, 1970.

(The Civilization of the American Indian Series) " . . . more than two hundred indigeneous drugs which were used by one or more Indian tribes have been official in *The Pharmacopeia of the United States of America* for varying periods since the first edition appeared in 1820, or in the *National Formulary* since it began in 1888" (p. 6).

Filled with anecdotes and accounts by the early European observers (colonists, traders, botanists, explorers, and missionaries), Vogel focuses not on the ritual aspect of Indian curing procedures but on the rational aspect, that is primarily on the knowledge the Indians had of the healing properties of native plants.

He describes the use of rotten grains of corn, dried and beaten to a powder, to cure an ulcer on a leg; the bark of the (probably) white pine to cure scurvy; the use of dried kelp to prevent goiter; the use of dogwood and other bark as a febrifuge; and so on.

Other Indian medical practices: sweat baths; the use of the enema (an animal bladder and a hollow bone); ways of removing bullets; antidotes for snakebites; childbirth customs; diet; and much more are all discussed in detail in this clearly written work based on a doctoral dissertation.

A 148-page appendix lists by common name – adder's tongue to vanilla bean – official botanical drugs used by North American Indians and cites the literature reporting this use.

A lengthy bibliography concludes the work which is the starting place for any student of Indian medical practices.

Barrow, Mark V. *Health and Disease of American Indians North of Mexico, a Bibliography, 1800–1969.* Compiled and edited by Mark V. Barrow, Jerry D. Niswander, and Robert Fortuine. Gainesville, Fla.: University of Florida Press, 1972.

Well described by its title, this is an unannotated list of 1,483 books, journal articles, and government documents, arranged by disease categories (infectious agents and diseases, neoplasms, mental health and psychiatric disorders, diseases of the digestive system, and so on). It does not include publications concerning Indian beliefs about medicine, or about medicine men or folk remedies.

There is an author, subject, and tribal index.

Kelso, Dianne R., and Carolyn L. Attneave, comps. *Bibliography of North American Indian Mental Health.* Westport, Conn. Greenwood Press, 1981.

(Prepared under the auspices of the White Cloud Center.)

Here is a computer-produced work which lists 1,363 documents published in the last eighty years in primarily anthropological and historical publications, and especially since the 1960s, also in medicine, psychiatry, social work, education and social and behavioral science publications.

Indians, Aleuts, Eskimos, and Metis are all covered.

Most of the citations are from refereed journals. The rest are from unpublished research reports, government documents, dissertations, papers presented at professional meetings, and individually authored chapters in books.

The subject (i.e., descriptor) index includes terms particularly appropriate to Indian study—Arctic hysteria, Windigo psychosis, witchcraft, ghost sickness, soul loss, taboo-breaking. It includes also terms expressive of norms or values of some Indian tribes which the glossary calls "Native American coping behavior" (e.g., noncompetitiveness, passive resistance, cooperation)—as well as, of course, terms of negative behavior shared with the dominant culture such as suicide, alcohol use, etc.

Front matter includes an introduction which discusses publishing trends in mental health research concerning Indians; a user's guide; a glossary; and a culture area and tribe list.

(*The American Indian Annotated Bibliography of Mental Health Volume I*, ERIC ED #151153, by these same two compilers has the first 500 citations listed here. In the ERIC document the first 250 entries also have abstracts).

Subject headings: "Indians of North America – Disease"; "Indians of North America – Health and Hygiene"; "Indians of North America – Medicine."

## History

Prucha, Francis Paul. *A Bibliographical Guide to the History of Indian-White Relations in the United States.* Chicago: University of Chicago Press, 1977.

_____. *Indian-White Relations in the United States, a Bibliography of Works Published 1975-1980.* Lincoln: University of Nebraska Press, 1982.

The first voluminous and informative work here lists 9,705 books, journal articles, dissertations, catalogs, and indexes covering from colonial times to the present. The titles are arranged into sections covering Indian policy, treaties, military relations, trade, missions, education, health, development, individual tribes, photographs of Indians, contributions to American life, capitivities, and on and on. Subsections entitled "Current Comment" record articles by the contemporaneous press on the event recorded. The chapters have paragraph introductions, and many of the sections also have brief notes placing the material in historical or comparative context: "The Moravians were among the most zealous of Protestant groups in missionary activity among Indians and produced outstanding leaders in the work like David Zeisberger and John Heckewelder" (p. 219); "Helen Hunt Jackson, a minor literary figure, became interested in Indian reform in 1879 . . . and devoted the remaining six years of her life to Indian affairs" (p. 63); "The Indians could not escape contacts with blacks as well as whites. These relationships have been of varied kinds – from use of black slaves by Indians before the Civil War to joining in protests against white society in recent times . . . [H]ere are studies that deal with aspects of Indian-black relations in the United States" (p. 352), etc.

The supplement follows a similar arrangement although it does not have nearly as many of the informative notes. It adds another 3,400 items, giving an idea of the immense amount of writing about Indians in the 1975-1980 period.

Both volumes have subject and tribal indexes.

Subject headings: "Indians of North America – Government Relations"; "Indians of North America – History."

## Journalism

Murphy, James Emmett, and Sharon M. Murphy. *Let My People*

*Know: American Indian Journalism, 1828–1978.* Norman: University of Oklahoma Press, 1981.

"By the 150th year of Indian journalism, the number of newspapers, newsletters, and periodicals of every sort had grown to nearly four hundred. Regularly scheduled Indian-managed or Indian-oriented programming was being carried by about one hundred radio stations and a handful of television stations. Satellite tele-communications projects were moving beyond the proposal state" (p. xx).

A fine, readable history of Indian newspapers and periodicals beginning with the founding of the *Cherokee Phoenix* in 1828 and ending with chapters on radio broadcasting in Indian country and the move toward Indian media associations (most notably the American Indian Press Association which was active from 1970 to 1975).

Covered are treatment of American Indians by the nation's mass media (briefly) and Indian journalism itself, including agency and mission publications, national, tribal and intertribal publications, regional papers and magazines, and specialized publications.

Appendixes include a directory of United States Indian newspapers and magazines and radio and television stations; Indian press freedom guarantees (from the *American Indian Civil Rights Handbook*); and "'An Address to the Whites' delivered by Elias Boudinot, a Cherokee Indian.'" (Boudinot was the first editor of the *Phoenix*, which was published in English and in the Cherokee syllabary invented by Sequoyah.)

The foreword is by Jeanette Henry, editor of the *Indian Historian.*

Subject headings: "Indian newspapers"; "Indian periodicals"; "Indians of North America — Mass media."

### Land

Sutton, Imre. *Indian Land Tenure: Bibliographical Essays and a Guide to the Literature.* New York: Clearwater, 1975.

Sutton "seeks to demonstrate how land tenure permeates virtually everything identified as Indian" and with this book gives a benchmark guide to the anthropology, geography, historical,and legal literature which is concerned with this subject. More than 1,000 citations follow background essays on aboriginal occupancy, land cessions and the establishment of reservations, colonial land policies, western expansion, the Indian Claims Commission, cattlemen, railroads, land allotment, heirship and alienation, water rights, treaty rights, hunting territories, and so on.

Subject headings: "Indians of North America—Claims"; "Indians of North America—Land tenure"; "Indians of North America—Land transfer."

## Language

Campbell, Lyle, and Marianne Mithun. *The Languages of Native America: Historical and Comparative Assessment.* Austin: University of Texas Press, 1979.

A long introduction, "North American Indian Historical Linguistics in Current Perspective," (by the two editors) sets the background for this volume of nineteen papers drawn from a conference held at Oswego, New York, in 1976. The papers report the status, as of the mid-1970s, of the study of the history of North American Indian language families. (Sample titles: "Timucua and Yuchi: Two Language Isolates of the Southeast," by James M. Crawford; "The Languages of South Texas and the Lower Rio Grande," by Ives Goddard; "The Kiowa-Tanoan, Keresan, and Zuni Languages," by Irvine Davis, "Na-Dene and Eskimo-Aleut," by Michael E. Krauss; etc.)

Each paper has an extensive bibliography, and there is an index to language names.

The concluding chapter, which suggests further research needs, is by Eric P. Hamp.

Despite the title, the book, which is reproduced from typescript, is limited to Central and North America.

Sebeok, Thomas A., ed. *Native Languages of the Americas* 2 vols. New York: Plenum Press, 1976–1977.

The state-of-the-art of North American Indian language studies as of about 1970. All of the contributors are recognized scholars. Chapters in Volume I include "History of American Indian Linguistics," by Harry Hoijer; "American Indian Linguistic Prehistory," by Mary R. Haas; "North American Indian Language Contact," by William Bright; "Philological Approaches to the Study of North American Indian Language: Documents and Documentation," by Ives Goddard; "Native North America," by Herbert Landar (discusses major historical figures such as Duponceau, Gallatin, etc., and institutions such as American Philosophical Society, the Smithsonian, etc., which figure historically in American Indian linguistic studies); and "Areal Linguistics in North America," by Joel Sherzer.

Other chapters, of varying lengths, focus on regions or languages stocks: Eskimo-Aleut; Na-Dene; the Northwest; California; Southwestern and Great Basin Languages; Algonquian; Siouian, Iroquoian, and Caddoan; and the Southeast.

Volume II of this set which is otherwise primarily on Central and South America has the nearly 200-page checklist "North American Indian Languages" by Herbert Landar.

This set has a complicated bibliographic history. All but one of the chapters in Volume I first appeared in Mouton and Company's series *Current Trends in Linguistics* Volume X, Linguistics of North America, copyright 1973. The exception, Landar's "Native North America," first appeared in *Current Trends in Linguistics* Volume XIII, *Historiography of Linguistics,* copyright 1975.

An earlier version of Landar's checklist, which is in Volume II of the Plenum set also, first appeared in Volume X of the Mouton series under a slightly different title, "The Tribes and Languages of North America: a Checklist."

Readers who want to read these chapters in the Mouton series should note that Volume X of *CTIL* was itself divided into four parts (in two physical volumes). *Native Languages of North America* is "Part 3"—the last section of Volume I and the first section of Volume II—of Volume X.

*Bibliography of Language Arts Materials for Native North Americans: Bilingual, English as a Second Language and Native Language Materials 1965-1974.* G. Edward Evans, Karin Abbey, and Dennis Reed. Los Angeles: American Indian Studies Center, University of California, 1977.

" . . . the Economic Opportunity Act of 1964 . . . designated that English must be taught as a Second Language to children for whom English was not a native language, and Indian schools should help transmit Indian culture" (p. 13-14).

The intent of this bibliography is to list the dictionaries, grammars, primers, alphabet books, storybooks, and adult reading materials which may be used in native language education, bilingual education, or English-as-a-Second-Language programs. Titles listed here were produced or reproduced between 1965 and 1974, years directly following the passage of the Bilingual Education Act when there was a large increase in production of these kinds of materials.

The introduction briefly treats the history of United States government policy, for and against, the teaching of Indian languages in the schools, including ways of writing them such as Sequoyah's Cherokee syllabary and James Evan's Cree syllabary. There is also a chart of the 108 extant Indian languages, giving the location where spoken, tribal population, number of speakers, and the number of titles for each language which are listed in this particular bibliography.

The book also includes a list, with addresses, of workers in bilingual and native language education and appendixes which cite general English-as-a-Second-Language materials, and critiques and evaluations of materials developed for, or useful in, language learning.

There is a total of 1,007 items in this bibliography.

Evans, G. Edward, and Jeffrey Clark. *North American Indian Language Materials, 1890–1965, an Annotated Bibliography of Monographic Works.* American Indian Bibliographic Series No. 3. Los Angeles: American Indian Studies Center, University of California, 1980.

From Aleut to Zuni – 187 dictionaries, grammars, orthographies, primers, readers, and the like. To be listed here they must be more than forty-nine pages in length and be published between 1890 and 1964. This list is designed to fill the gap between James C. Pilling's nine linguistic bibliographies which appeared in the United States *Bureau of American Ethnology Bulletins* and covered nineteenth-century material and the Evans and Abbey bibliography which covers the post-1965 period.

(Both books are reproduced from typescript and reasonably priced. The Evans and Clark book cost $3.00 on publication, and the Evans and Abbey book cost $4.00).

Subject headings: "Indians of North America – Languages." Subject headings for a particular language are, for example, "Cherokee language"; "Crow language"; "Mohawk language"; etc. (See also Marken, Jack. *The American Indian: Language and Literature,* in the Literature Section.)

Journal:    *International Journal of American Linguistics* v. 1, 1917–
University of Chicago Press
5801 Ellis Ave.
Chicago, IL 60637

## Law

Cohen, Felix S. *Handbook of Federal Indian Law.* Albuquerque: Unviersity of New Mexico Press, 1971.

"Long out of print since it was originally published in 1942 by the U.S. Government Printing Office, this classic work on Federal Indian law, and the whole legal history of Indian-white relations, is here republished in a facsimile edition. It is, as Felix Frankfurter observed, the only book that has ever made sense and order from 'the vast hodgepodge of treaties, statutes, judicial and administrative rulings, and unrecorded practice in which the intricacies and perplexities, confusions and injustices of the law governing Indians lay concealed'" (publishers note, p. xviii).

A new foreword, a biography, and a bibliography, of Felix Cohen precedes this reprint which is exactly as Felix Cohen wrote it and which should not be confused with the rewritten version which was favorable to termination and which was issued by the Government Printing Office in 1958.

Getches, David H., Daniel M. Rosenfelt, and Charles F. Wilkinson. *Cases and Materials on Federal Indian Law.* St. Paul: West Publishing Co., 1979.

" 'Traditional Indian strictures and their modern counterparts in tribal constitutions and codes are "Indian laws" but they are not the primary concern of federal Indian law. The field of federal Indian law involves that body of law which regulates the legal relationships between Indian tribes and the United States . . . "

"The body of federal Indian law—expressed in separate volumes of the United States Code and the Code of Federal Regulations, in some 380 treaties, in hundreds of opinions of the Solicitor of the Department of the Interior, in thousands of cases, and in scores of law review articles—is expanding rapidly. Each year the Supreme Court decides more Indian cases than the numbers of Indians relative to the population as a whole would seem to justify. This suggests two significant points, both accurate: First, the interests and rights of more than Indians are concerned. Second, Indians, more than any other ethnic group, are subject to extensive legal regulation" (p. xvii).

This book is designed for law school students. Chapter headings are: "Indians and Indian Law"; "The History of Federal Policy toward American Indians"; "The Bureau of Indian Affairs"; "The Federal-Tribal Relationship"; "Tribal Sovereignty, Federal Supremacy, and States Right"; "Tribal Self-Government"; "Jurisdiction in Indian Country"; "The Rights of Individual Indians"; "Indian Lands"; "Water Rights"; and "Fishing and Hunting Rights."

There is a detailed table of contents, a table of statutes, and a table of cases.

Although primarily for law school students, much material of interest to anthropologists, social workers, historians, or any student of United States social and political problems which relates to Indians appear here.

Price, Monroe E. *Law and the American Indian. Readings, Notes and Cases.* Indianapolis: Bobbs-Merrill, 1973.

This first-ever casebook on Indian law was intended to complement Felix Cohen's *Handbook of Federal Indian Law*; to encourage the study of Indian legal problems; to serve as a coursebook for students studying the legal context of American Indian history; and to provide practical and useful material for Indian people and their lawyers.

The five chapters are: "Sovereignty and the Flow of Power"; "The Power of the States"; "Concepts of Property in Federal Indian Law"; "Land Tenure, Land Use, and Economic Development"; and "Strengthening Tribal Government." Each chapter has a brief introduction and is comprised of cases and notes. The notes are historical source materials, government memoranda, and relevant excerpts from books or journal articles by anthropologists, economists, historians, etc. There is a detailed table of contents, a table of cases, and a bibliography of law review articles relating to Indian affairs which is arranged by subjects such as custom and law; fishing and hunting rights; Indians of Canada; tribal governments; water law; and so forth.

Gasaway, Laura N., James L. Hoover, and Dorothy M. Warden. *American Indian Legal Materials: A Union List.* Stanfordville, N.Y.: Earl M. Coleman, 1980.

A union list is a compilation of titles from more than one library. This particular list is of American Indian legal materials held by twenty-eight law libraries (twenty-five university law libraries, the Department of Interior Natural Resources Library, and the library of the law firm of Wilkinson, Cragun and Baker).

It includes 4,545 unannotated items. They are monographs, government documents, and serial titles (but not individual periodical articles), and there are indexes by subject, geographic region, and tribe.

The compilers say that each contributing library identified its own American Indian titles, so that ethnology, education and even fiction titles were submitted.

As Professor Rennard Strickland cautions in the foreword, this book is limited to materials drawn from law libraries, and students of Indian law, history, and policy will often need to look beyond the law library to special collections, which house rare materials, and to non-legal libraries. He notes at the beginning of his foreword that "no jurisprudential field crosses more disciplines than American Indian law. Nowhere else is there such a practical and scholarly need to borrow from history and economics and anthropology and geography and education and biology and business and engineering."

This is a useful starting place for legal research.

Subject headings: "Indians of North America—Courts"; "Indians of North America—Government relations"; "Indians of North America—Legal status, laws, etc."; "Indians of North America—Tribal government." (See also the Treaty section.)

Journals:    *American Indian Journal.* v. 1, 1972–
Institute for the Development of Indian Law
927 15th St., N.W., Suite 200
Washington, DC 20005

*Announcements, Native American Rights Fund.*
v. 1, 1972–
Native American Rights Fund
1506 Broadway
Boulder, CO  80302

## *Libraries*

Townley, Charles T. "American Indian Library Service." Vol. 8 in *Advances in Librarianship,* ed. Harris, Michael H., pp. 135–180. New York: Academic Press, 1978.

Townley surveys the status of library service to the Indian people of the United States as of the 1970s (describing the Indian target population as that of a young, rapidly growing ethnic group with high rates of unemployment, alcoholism, mental illness, and functional English illiteracy); gives background information on community, school, postsecondary, and research libraries for Indians prior to 1973 (there wasn't much); and then describes specific library projects as of 1973 and later. These include the Rough Rock Community School Library, the Standing Rock Tribal Library, the Akwesasne Library Culture Center, the Sioux City Public Library Indian Library Project, and more.

Some of the findings he reports are: Indian communities have special information needs – reservation communities want information on their own tribe, urban communities want information on many tribes, children need cultural and curriculum-related information, teenagers want vocational information, and adults want practical and cultural information that will improve their quality of life. Further, the demand for information is increasing, and Indian control of their own libraries is essential as library services established without community input and approval will be regarded as an insult (p. 170). There is also a need for Indian library professionals; for in-service training and for continuing education of library staff with a "career ladder" available to the staff.

A good bibliography on Indians and libraries as of the 1970s concludes the article.

Journal:    *American Indian Libraries Newsletter*. v. 1, 1976–
            American Library Association
            50 E. Huron St.
            Chicago, IL 60611

## *Literature*

Hobson, Geary, ed. *The Remembered Earth, an Anthology of Contemporary Native American Literature.* Albuquerque: University New Mexico Press, 1981.

Originally published in 1979 by Red Earth Press, Albuquerque, New Mexico.)

There are all forms of literature here – lots of good, evocative poetry, short and long, on themes as varied as religion, drunkenness, nature, family, hunting. There are chapters from novels-in-progress, including Larry Emerson's "Gallup." There is reportage; Simon Ortiz's "We Shall Endure," an account of a march in Gallup in support of Wounded Knee 1973. There is social comment; Geary Hobson's "The Rise of the White Shaman as a New Version of Cultural Imperialsim" (taking pot shots at the white poets who think they can become Indian-like shamans). There are short stories, including Leslie Marmon Silko's raw, strong "Storyteller." There is a play, Geraldine Keams's "The Flight of the Army Worm." There is Paula Gunn Allen's "The Sacred Hoop: A Contemporary Indian Perspective on American Indian Literature" which is just that. And there is brief biographical information on each of the seventy-three contributors—tribal affiliation, publications, where they were born, live, and work.

This is a book with lots of verve which would probably appeal more to young readers than the old Indian legends which sometimes suffer from a murky translation.

Levitas, Gloria, Frank Robert Vivelo, and Jacqueline J. Vivelo. *American Indian Prose and Poetry, We Wait in the Darkness.* New York; G. P. Putnam's Sons, Capricorn Books, 1974.

This assemblage of poems, legends, love charms, origin tales, moral lessons, and nature stories is arranged chronologically—Before the Coming of the White Man, After the White Man Came, The Present—within the chronological divisions by culture area (Northwest Coast, Plateau, California, Great Basin, Southwest, Plains, Prairies, East Subarctic, and Eastern) and within these areas by tribe.

The entries vary from one-half to six pages in length, and in the first two sections, are drawn mainly from the old Bureau of American Ethnology publications and other standard anthropological classics. The third and much smaller section is composed primarily of poetry from sources such as the periodical *Akwesasne Notes.*

The introduction theorizes on the relationship between the economy and social structure of a tribe and the kind of literature it produced. Thus, the Pueblos, a village people, emphasized complex ritual poetry spoken by a priest with the community present while the hunting societies of the Plains, Plateau, and Prairie tended to be more individualistic, with brief love songs and hunting songs. What group rituals they had were also briefer.

A chart at the end of the introduction lists the tribes, their "techno-economic level" (hunters-gatherers, or farmers), their culture area, and their language family.

Sample titles are "The Rabbit Who Stole the Fire" (Seminole); "I Sit Here Thinking of Her"(Ojibwa); "The Boy Who Caught the Sun" (Assiniboine); "Star Husband" (Coast Salish); "I Am the Master of Life" (Delaware); "All is Trouble Along the Klamath" (Yurok); "Our Word for the White Man is Wasi' chu" [greedy].

Witt, Shirley Hill, and Stan Steiner. *The Way, an Anthology of American Indian Literature.* New York: Alfred A. Knopf, 1972.

There are two kinds of writing in this anthology of about 130 pieces. The first kind is composed of the small classics of Indian oratory. There is Chief Joseph's "I Will Fight No More Forever"; Red Jacket's reply to the Reverend Cram, (" . . . Brother: You say there is but one religion, why do you white people differ so much about it? Why are not all agreed, as you can all read the book?); Chief Seathe's (Seattle's) warning when he gave up his tribe's land, (" . . . At night when the streets of your cities and villages shall be silent, and you think them deserted, they will throng with the returning hosts that once filled and still love this beautiful land . . . ".

The second kind of writing included here is contemporary. There are excerpts from newspapers, children's school compositions, poetry, jokes, political and social comment – all by Indians reflecting of the humor and misery of coexistence with white people in the United States of America in the twentieth century.

Sample titles are: "On an Indian Reservation: How Colonialism Works"; "Manifest Destiny: Vietnam and the Indians"; "Too Many Scientists and Not Enough Chiefs" (on anthropologists and others who study Indians); "I Am a Papago Girl"; "The Lost Brother: an Iroquois Prophecy of the Serpent"; "The Voice of the American Indian, Declaration of Indian Purpose, American Indian Chicago Conference"; "Red Power: an Eight Point Program"; and so on.

None of the writings included here is more than a few pages in length, and the whole is preceded by an introduction by the first editor, Shirley Witt.

Jacobson, Angeline. *Contemporary Native American Literature: a Selected and Partially Annotated Bibliography*. Metuchen, N.J.: Scarecrow Press, 1977.

Lists 1,649 individual poems by native authors. ("Native American" in this book includes Eskimo, Canadian, and Mexican tribal writers as well as United States Indians.) Also included are some 375 works on the native American spiritual heritage (primarily retold myths and legends), book-length fiction, autobiography, biography, letters, interviews, humor, anthologies, bibliographies and indexes, and so on. All of the titles, except the individual poems, have informative annotations. There is an author index as well as a title and first-line index (to the poems).

The emphasis is on works written between 1960 and mid-1976, but there are some older titles, particularly in the autobiography section.

Lass-Woodfin, Mary Jo, ed. *Books on American Indians and Eskimos, a Selection Guide for Children and Young Adults*. Chicago: American Library Association, 1978.

In this guide to literature for children, Lass-Woodfin rates 807 books for elementary school and up. A thought-provoking introduction which discusses among other problems those raised by books which stereotype in a positive manner, "'Pueblo Indians are a gentle, kindly, laughter-loving people,'" is followed by an overview of the various types of literature—fiction, nonfiction, autobiography, biography, legends, myths, poetry, and captivity stories. The full-paragraph annotations are both descriptive and evaluative and conclude with "good," "adequate," or "poor—think before buying, seriously flawed in writing and/or accuracy . . . ." (There are no wishy-washy recommendations in this book.)

Grade-level estimates are also given so that a teacher, parent, or librarian can choose a book appropriate to the child's reading ability, and the detailed subject index cites specific pages in a book if the book covers more than one subject or tribe.

Marken, Jack W. *The American Indian: Language and Literature.* Arlington Heights, Ill.: AHM Publishing Corp., 1978.

Goldentree bibliographies in language and literature.

*The American Indian: Language and Literature* is an unannotated list of 3,695 books and journal articles on Indian languages, linguistics, sign language, myths, tales, legends, writings by Indian authors (both literary and nonliterary), and "critical discussions" of Indian literature. (This last includes criticism of works about Indians by non-Indians, e.g., critiques of James Fenimore Cooper's books.)

Works the compiler considers especially important as well as those available in paperback are so indicated, and an index provides access by author, tribe, and language name and also gives tribal identification if the author is an Indian.

The compiler says that "some journals accessible only in the largest libraries have been omitted," but his abbreviations list, which includes journals and monographic series, has 378 titles in it, leading to the conclusion that not many journals were omitted.

A work daunting in its comprehensiveness, this is a valuable and time-saving compilation for students in this field.

Stensland, Anna Lee. *Literature by and about the American Indian: an Annotated Bibliography for Junior and Senior High Schools Students.* Urbana, Ill.: National Council of Teachers of English, 1973.

Stensland includes anthropological, historical, and sociological books about the Indian, but as befits a book published by the

National Council of Teachers of English, emphasizes legends, poetry, fiction, and biography since, the compiler says, that is what the teacher of English needs. Her annotations give a brief summary, mentioning good points and drawbacks and telling something about the author when possible. They may also include quotes from American Indian critics or simply note that the book appeared in an Indian-sponsored bibliography.

Stensland concludes with study guides to nine of the titles listed; capsule biographies of twenty-five of the most prolific Indian scholars and writers; lists of basic books for a collection for a junior high-school library and for a senior high-school library; addresses of sources of additional material; a directory of publishers; an author and a title index.

Definitely a worthwhile book, this itself belongs in a list of basic books for a collection on the American Indian.

Stensland, Anna Lee. *Literature by and about the American Indian*: *an Annotated Bibliography*. Urbana, Ill.: National Council of Teachers of English, 1979.

Nearly 800 titles are in this second edition of Stensland which differs from the first in that it identifies books for children of elementary school age as well as for junior and senior high-school students, and also has some Canadian, Alaskan, and Mexican literature (unlike the first edition which concentrated on books about Indians living in the area which is now the lower forty-eight United States.)

The introduction briefly discusses some of the recurring themes in literature about Indians: betrayal by whites, the spirituality of life, loyalty to the tribe, women of bravery, the sacredness of nature, the captive white child, and also discusses some recurring Indian stereotypes in literature: the noble red man, the heathen savage, murderous thieves, idlers and drunkards, the beautiful maiden, the vanishing race, and the faithful friend and servant.

Like the first edition this volume may quote Indian critiques of a book or note that the work appears in an Indian-sponsored bibliography. (Some of these assessments are not favorable.)

There are also capsule biographies of fifty-four writers considered to be Indian.

Subject headings: "Indians of North America – Literary collections"; "Indians of North America – Juvenile literature"; "Indian literature – North America"; "Indian literature – Translations into English"; "American literature – Translations from Indian languages"; "American literature – Indian authors."

Journals:    *Blue Cloud Quarterly.* v. 1, 1954–
Benet Tvedten
Marvin, SD 57251

*Suntracks.* v. 1, 1975–
Dept. of English
University of Arizona
Tucson, AZ 85721

*Tawow: Canadian Indian Cultural Magazine.*
v. 1, 1970–
Dept. of Indian and Northern Affairs
Indian Cultural Identity Division
10 Wellington St.
Hull, P. Q.
(Subs. to Supply and Services Canada, Publg.
Center. Hull, P. Q. K1A OS9)

## Missions

Bowden, Henry Warner. *American Indians and Christian Missions, Studies in Cultural Conflict.* Chicago History of American Religion. Chicago: University of Chicago Press, 1981.

In seven short chapters Bowden (1) reviews the pre-Columbian civilization; (2, 3, and 4) describes the representative Indian cultures (Tewa, Huron, and Massachuset tribes which correspond to areas of early Spanish, French, and English contact); and (5, 6, and 7) summarizes mission activity of the eighteenth, nineteenth, and twentieth centuries. Discussed here is the difference in approach of the Protestant and Catholic missionaries; the differences, too, of the religious beliefs and of the cultures of the tribes who were subjected to the missionaries' labors. Many of the big names of mission history are here: John Eliot, David and John Brainerd, Samuel Kirkland, David Zeisberger, and Isaac McCoy. Mentioned as well are the individual ceremonies: the Delaware Big House ceremony, the Cherokee Green Corn Festival, the Dakota Sun Dance, and more, onto the present-day Native American (Peyote) Church.

This is a successful introduction to a vast and potentially emotional subject written at a time when, as Martin E. Marty notes in his foreword, "most Americans have lost faith in the attempt to convert Indians, a time when they have come to respect the integrity of native American faith, to see missionary efforts as intrusive and to regard 'civilizing' efforts as condescending" (p. xii).

The book concludes with a nine-page bibliographical essay "Suggestions for Further Reading."

Ronda, James P., and James Axtell. *Indian Missions, a Critical Bibliography*. Newberry Library Center for the History of the American Indian Bibliographic Series. Bloomington: Indiana University Press, 1978.

Introducing their book, Ronda and Axtell note that as Europeans invaded the Indian domain, missionaries were nearly always in the vanguard and their efforts influenced the behavior of both Indians and Europeans in many ways. The missionaries wanted a cultural revolution for the American Indians. They hoped by their labors to bring it about, and because they were "skilled propagandists, scholars have allowed their words – from mission reports, relations, letters, pamphlets, and autobiographies to dominate our understanding of the mission . . . [and] an ethnocentric perspective, with its harsh rhetoric of civilization-versus savagery, pervaded Indian mission writing well into the present century" (p. 2). It is only in the past twenty years that "history has begun to replace hagiography in the study of Indian missions" . . . [and become] "less interested in the number of mission buildings" and "more concerned with the cultural interaction that took place within [them]" (p. 3). Scholars are now attempting "to restore Indian words and actions to their rightful place . . . . Traditional mission history simply ignored them" (p. 4).

Following the standard format of the Newberry Library Center for the History of the American Indian Bibliographical Series, this little book lists works recommended for the beginner and for a basic library collection.

The bibliography itself has 221 books and articles. (Items suitable for secondary students are so designated.) It is preceded by a fine fifty-page bibliographical essay which gives background information on missionary activities to the Indians in North America and then reviews in a few paragraphs or pages the major writings on each denomination's activities: Anglican and Episcopal; Baptists; Catholic; Methodist; Moravian; Mormon; Presbyterian and American Board; and Quaker. (Also discussed are works on mission goals, mission towns, conversion, etc.)

Subject heading: "Indians of North America – Missions."

### *Motion Pictures*

Bataille, Gretchen M., and Charles L. P. Silet. *The Pretend Indians,*

*Images of Native Americans in the Movies.* Ames, Iowa: Iowa State University Press, 1980.

A collection of articles and reviews, previously printed in journals and books, on Indians as portrayed in movies. (The first section is entitled "The Native American: Myth and Media Stereotyping.") Selections range in time from "The 'Make-Believe' Indian" *Moving Picture World,* 8 (4 March, 1911) to *"Little Big Man:* the Novel and the Film," *Literature/Film Quarterly* 5 (Spring 1977). Authors include Vine Deloria, Leslie Fiedler, Stanley Vestal, Dan Georgakas, Richard Schickel, etc., and there is a short selection of pictures from films beginning with 1920, the *Last of the Mohicans* (Wallace Beery played Magua), to 1975, *Buffalo Bill and the Indians or Sitting Bull's History Lesson.*

The final chapter is a seventeen-page annotated checklist of articles and books on the popular image of Indians in American films.

Fascinating.

Subject heading: "Indians in motion pictures."

## Music

Densmore, Frances. *The American Indians and Their Music.* New York: The Womans Press, 1926. Reprint. New York: Johnson Reprint Corporation, 1970.

According to Frances Densmore, Indian singing begins high, ends low, and has more rhythm than melody. It is accompanied by percussion instruments and is more often a man's than a woman's occupation. (A leading singer may know up to 400 songs.)

Densmore, who died in 1957, was the major figure in American Indian music studies for nearly fifty years. Here, in an informal style, she gives introductory information on Indian home life, languages, arts and crafts, and so on, and then sketches the "why" of Indian songs: the function of music was religious. Songs were used to treat the sick or to ensure success in war, in hunting, or in games. She also gives examples, with words and music, of kinds of songs — those received in dreams, bought from their owners, inherited, sung to praise or to honor another, and so on.

Other chapters give information on the two kinds of musical instruments: wind (flute and whistles) and percussion (drums and rattles); on how they are made; and on how they are used. There is also a discussion of earlier books and scholars in the field of American Indian music.

This small book which originally appeared in 1926, in its reprinted version remains in print today.

Nettl, Bruno. *North American Indian Musical Styles*. Memoirs of the American Folklore Society, Volume 45. Philadelphia: American Folklore Society, 1954.

In the usual style of a doctoral dissertation published as one of the memoirs of the American Folklore Society and also in three installments of the *Journal of American Folklore*, 67, 1954, Bruno Nettl briefly covers the history of the study of North American Indian music, critiquing earlier scholars and their works, and then surveys the musical styles (by kinds of melody, rhythm, song form, vocal techniques used, etc.) for about eighty tribes, using as material music recorded after about 1880.

Doing this, Nettl divides Indian music into six musical areas and lists the important traits for each area. The musical areas he identifies are Eskimo-Northwest; Great Basin; California-Yuman; Athabascan: Plains-Pueblo; and Eastern area.

"North America. Indian and Eskimo Influence," Vol. 13 in *The New Grove Dictionary of Music and Musicians*. Pp. 295–320. London: Macmillan, 1980.

"In many Indian cultures there was very little music that did not accompany dancing, and the structure of the music was sometimes closely related to that of the dance" (p. 297).

Here is an encyclopedia article covering dance as well as music written by such well-known ethnomusicologists as Willard Rhodes, Bruno Nettl, Gertrude Kurath, etc., based on their own fieldwork and on the standard published sources.

The music section traces the history of the study of American Indian music; discusses the various styles, generally and by region (the Plains, the East, the Southwest, the Great Basin, the Northwest coast, and the North); describes the various influence; peyote music; the Ghost Dance; and Pan-Indian influences. The dance section discusses the religious purposes of dance, the symbolism and elements of style, the relation of dance to music, such modern versions as fiesta and powwow dancing, and concludes with sections on various tribes: Blackfoot, Chippewa, Iroquois, Kwakiutl, Paiute, Papago, Seminole, Tewa, and Wabanaki. Eskimo dance is also covered.

Each major section has a bibliography.

Haywood, Charles. *A Bibliography of North American Folklore and Folksong*. 2d rev. ed. 2 vols. New York: Dover Publications, 1961.

"This new Dover edition first published in 1961, is an unabridged and corrected republication of the work first published by Greenberg Publisher in 1951, to which has been added a new Index Supplement: Composers, Arrangers, Performers.

The First edition of this work appeared in one volume, but this Dover edition is published in two volumes." (p. iv)

Volume Two of this set has the title "American Indians North of Mexico Including the Eskimos" and is divided into two parts. Part One is a general bibliography—folklore, music, dance, musical arrangements, and recordings (i.e., for Indians in general), and Part Two is the bibliography by culture areas. The culture areas are Northeastern, Southeastern, the Plains, Southwestern, California, the Great Basin, the Plateau, the Northwest Coast, the Mackenzie-Yukon, and the Arctic Coast (Eskimo).

For each area general works for that particular region on folklore and music are listed; then the works on folklore and music for each tribe are listed. Divisions in the folklore sections are, normally, general studies; myths, tales, legends; beliefs; customs; folk medicine; folk art; speech; and games. Divisions in the music sections are general studies; dances; arrangements; and records.

There are perhaps 12,000 citations in this volume—to books, journal articles, musical arrangements, and musical recordings.

The amazing breadth of coverage here makes this useful for anthropologists and ethnologists as well as for students of folklore, music, and legends.

Subject heading: "Indians of North America—Music"; "Indians of North America—Dance."

### *Religion*

Gill, Sam D. *Native American Religions, an Introduction*. Belmont, Calif.: Wadsworth Publishing Co., 1982.

A title in the Religious Life of Man series, this book speaks to the wonderful complexity of North American Indian religions, discovering "aspects of religion in stories of creation, of heroes, of tricksters, of fools . . . in architecture, art, and orientations in the landscape . . . in ritual drama, costumes, masks, and ceremonial paraphernalia . . . related to hunting, farming, and fishing . . . [and] find[ing] grand cosmological schemes and religious ideas in the rudest, most common materials and circumstances as well as in highly developed poetic, intellectual, and artistic forms" (pp. 11–12).

For all of these aspects specific examples are given; the Zuni with their seven-part cosmological structure (the four directions, the zenith, the nadir, and the center); the hows and whys of Navajo sandpainting; the Hopi kachinas; the Seneca falsefaces; the Pueblo clowns; the Apache girls' puberty rites; the part played by the stories, songs, and poetry of many different tribes.

The final chapter discusses the present-day religions of the Rio Grande Pueblos and the Yaqui community of Arizona (blends of ancient Catholic and Indian practices) and of the Native American Church (the Peyote religion).

The author notes that he has not included or sought information traditionally kept secret and that his goals with this book have been to furnish an introduction to Native American religion as a field in religious studies.

Footnotes at the end of each chapter cite the major primary sources for the study of Indian religions and there are "Suggestions for Further Reading."

Hultkrantz, Ake. *The Religions of the American Indian*. Translated by Monica Setterwall. Berkeley: University of California Press, 1979.

Originally published as *De Amerikanska Indianernas Religioner*, 1967.)

_____. *Belief and Worship in Native North America*. Edited by Christopher Vecsey. Syracuse: Syracuse University Press, 1981.

There are two books here from the Professor of Comparative Religion and Head of the Institute of Comparative Religion, University of Stockholm.

The first — translated from the Swedish and reading like it — covers the tribal religions of North America, the "high" religions of South and Central America (i.e., the religions of the Incas of Peru and the Aztecs and Mayans of Mexico which differ from the tribal religions in that they are "scripture" religions).

The author says in his preface that the "perspective in this work must be mainly typological and phenomenological . . . . Historical reconstructions are attempted and the main lines of the development of tribal Indian religions sketched" (pp. xii–xiii).

Part One of this first book, then, which is the section treating North America, has chapter titles such as "Totemism and Belief in

Guardian Spirits"; "Medicine Man and Shamans"; "The Great Tribal Ceremonies"; "The Soul and Life Hereafter"; and so on. In this book, Hultkrantz so frequently cites previous writers on the subject and provides such a large bibliography that this is a book as much on the *writings* about native American religion as on the religions themselves.

Still, the breadth of coverage here is astounding, and any serious student of North American Indian religions will want to study it.

The second book here is easier to read perhaps because it is a collection of fifteen articles published between 1954 and 1981 and is therefore by its nature meant to be read in shorter doses.

It is divided into four parts: "Belief and Myth"; "Worship and Ritual"; "Ecology and Religion"; and "Persistence and Change." Sample chapter titles are "The Structure of Theistic Beliefs among North American Plains Religion," "Spirit Lodge, a North American Shamanistic Seance," "Attitudes to Animals in Shoshoni Indian Religions," and "Conditions for the Spread of The Peyote Cult in North America."

Again, there is a long bibliography.

Hultkrantz has done brief stints of fieldwork among the Wind River Shoshoni and the Arapahoes of Wyoming and has written more than six books and 200 articles on American Indian religion. To this second book, Christopher Vecsey has contributed a sympathetic account of Hultkrantz's life — the life of a man who became interested in Indians as a boy growing up in Sweden and whose interest has persisted throughout his professional career.

Underhill, Ruth. *Red Man's Religion. Beliefs and Practices of the Indians North of Mexico*. Chicago: University of Chicago Press, 1965.

Writing with clarity, grace, and glints of humor, Ruth Underhill describes Indian beliefs and ceremonies as they were before white contact changed them (based on reports of the first white observers) and as she herself saw them in thirty years of living, working, and visiting with Indian tribes.

As, she says, there are already compilations of mythology or, from the Indian point of view, theology, *Red Man's Religion* concentrates on ceremonies, for it is the constantly held ceremonies, she believes, that are the essential in Indian religions. From the ceremony [Indians] "received security and courage, whereas the myth might be as vague as some fine points of theology are to the modern churchgoers" (p. 4). To Indians "there was no division between economic and religious life. . . . Ceremonies great and small were the very fabric of life. They furnished the chief opportunities for learning, for feasting, for lovemaking. They gave courage to the lone hunter. They fused a group together in heartening ritual. They combined the functions not only of a church but of a school, clinic, theater, and law court" (p. 5).

She also touches briefly on sorcery and witchcraft as part of religion; all power is one – it is the way it is used for good or evil that is the distinction.

Other topics covered include world origin beliefs; woman power; attitude toward the dead; medicine men, shamans, and priests; visions, hunting and gathering rituals; the Sun Dance; war ceremonies; and planting ceremonies. This last topic is divided by region, the Southern Woodlands; the Iroquois; the Great Lakes and Upper Mississippi; the Prairie; and the Puebloes.

There is also a chapter on modern religions.

Black-and-white illustrations and a long bibliography complete this, the most readable, of the general surveys of Indian religion.

Subject headings: "Indians of North America – Religion and Mythology"; "Indians of North America – Rites and Ceremonies"; also specific rites (e.g., "Sun-dance").

## Sociology

Thornton, Russell, and Mary K. Grasmick. *Sociology of American Indians, a Critical Bibliography*. Newberry Center for the History of the American Indian Bibliographic Series. Bloomington: Indiana University Press, 1980.

A recent survey of social science literature pertaining to the American Indian showed that the largest number of articles (several thousand) were published in anthropological journals; another 1,500 appeared in history journals. American studies, ethnic studies, and geography had about 100 each, and economics and political science had a few dozen each. There were about 300 in sociological journals (produced in the one-hundred-year history of sociology in the United States and Canada) (pp. 1–2).

This bibliography of 331 citations (a few books, mostly journal articles, no theses) is of that sociological literature. It is preceded by a bibliographical essay on the works which suggests the need for the study of American Indians by disciplines other than anthropology and history. "The preference in sociology for contemporary, urban societies is needed to complement both the chronological concerns of history and anthropology's emphasis on traditional and rural cultures . . . sociology's interest in the family unit is just as important as anthropology's interest in the kinship systems of American Indians, and sociology's concern with social stratification would provide new perspectives on past events in the history of American-Indian-White relations" (p. 5).

Topics covered in the bibliographical essay include demography (historical and contemporary); sociocultural change; religion and religious movements; relations with minority and majority groups; social stratification; economies; judicial systems; the family and sex roles; education; urbanization; and more.

Like all of the Newberry series this book identifies a few works "For the Beginner" and "For a Basic Library Collection," and indicates those works suitable for secondary school students.

### Treaties

*Indian Treaties and Surrenders, from 1680–1890.* 2 vols. Ottawa: Queen's Printer, 1891. Reprint. Toronto: Coles Publishing Co., 1971.

Kappler, Charles J., comp. *Indian Affairs Laws and Treaties.* 5 vols. Washington, D.C.: GPO, 1976.
   (Vol. 1, Laws, 1 Dec. 1902; vol. 2, Treaties, 1904; vol. 3, Laws, 1 Dec. 1913; vol. 4, Laws, 4 Mar. 1927; vol. 5, Laws, 29 June 1938.)

*Kappler's Indian Affairs: Laws and Treaties.* vol. 6, 7. Washington, D.C.: GPO, 1979.

Directly applicable to any question about treaties (who signed and what they signed), these immense volumes are the cornerstones for any study of the history of Indian-white relations in the United States and Canada.

Volume 2 of the Kappler work above was reprinted in 1975 as *Indian Treaties, 1778–1883* (1,099 p.) by Interland Publishing of New York. Volumes 6 and 7 supplement the previous five-volume work which contains treaties and statutes enacted through the 75th Congress extending the work through the 91st Congress, 1970.

The Canadian volumes have the added advantage of foldout maps.

Subject headings: "Indians of North America—Treaties"; "Indians of North America—Canada—Treaties." (See also the subject headings under Law.)

### Urban Indians

Sorkin, Alan L. *The Urban American Indian.* Lexington, Mass.: Lexington Books, D. C. Heath and Co., 1978.

Citing government documents, journal articles, mimeographed reports, etc., the author, an economics professor, discusses, theorizes, and draws his own conclusions about the problems which urban Indians face.

Some of his observations: The American Indian population is growing faster than any other group and now numbers about one million. Approximately one-half of this population now lives in urban areas compared to slightly more than one-fourth in 1960.

"In terms of labor force, status, income, and housing, reservation Indians are the most disadvantaged group in the United States" (p. 23).

From the early 1950s until 1972, the Bureau of Indian Affairs operated a training and relocation program placing reservation Indians in positions in major metropolitan areas. In 1972 the program changed with most participants being trained and getting jobs near the reservation and fewer being sent to the cities (p. 41).

Urban Indians tend to prefer daily pay jobs (p. 42).

The health of urban Indians . . . may be worse than the health of reservation Indians who receive comprehensive free medical services from the IHS (p. 63).

Alcoholism is a major problem and Indians will not respond to alcoholism programs in which the attending staff and patients are primarily non-Indian (p. 63).

Native Americans live in the worst housing in the worst areas of cities and tend to concentrate in particular sections of cities. This may help ease the transition from the reservation, but in the long run it may hinder economic adjustment (p. 83).

Indian students "may face prejudice and hostility from their fellow students, and teachers in metropolitan areas are generally unfamiliar with the problems of the urban Indian" (p. 104).

"These and other factors tend to cause poor achievement levels among native American students as well as high dropout rates. The latter occurs in spite of substantial evidence that urban Indian economic status is enhanced by completing secondary school" (p. 104).

"The development of Indian institutions and organizations typically goes through three stages: the bar culture, Indian centers and friendship networks, and finally the development of Pan-Indian ethnic institutions. Most cities with large Indian populations are probably in the second stage of institutional development" (p. 121).

"The uniqueness of reservation culture has made native American adjustment to urban society difficult and psychologically painful. Some traditional Indian values are simply incompatible with those of the dominant culture" (p. 136).

Waddell, Jack O., and O. Michael Watson. *The American Indian in Urban Society*. Boston: Little, Brown and Co., 1971.

In an attempt to provide source material on present-day Indians living in cities here is a collection of essays by ten authors (nine anthropologists and one American Indian social casework director) which tries to answer: the character, historically and currently, of the urbanization trends in America as they have affected Indians; the character of Indian participation in the social institutions found in the city; and why some Indians "succeed" in adapting to urban life and remain in the city, while others, even some who "succeed," decide to return to their largely rural home communities (pp. viii–ix). (Quotation marks in orginal.)

Sample chapter titles include "The Reservation Community and the Urban Community: Hopi Indians of Moenkopi" by Shuichi Nagata; "Life in the City: Chicago"; by Merwyn S. Garbarino; "Urban Economic Opportunities: the Example of Denver," by Robert S. Weppner; "Drinking and Drunkenness Among Urban Indians," by Theodore D. Graves; "Involvement in an Urban University," by Frank C. Miller; and "Epilogue: the Urban Indian as Viewed by an Indian Caseworker," by John W. Olson.


Thornton, Russell, Gary D. Sandefur, and Harold G. Grasmick. *The Urbanization of American Indians, a Critical Bibliography*. Newberry Library Center for the History of the American Indian Bibliographic Series. Bloomington: Indiana University Press, 1982.

In the standard form of the Newberry bibliographical series, this small book has a bibliographical essay, sketching the urban background of American Indians from the great pre-Columbian cities such as the Mesoamerican Teotihuacan, which may have had a population of 200,000, to the mid-twentieth-century rural-to-urban migration in the United States which means that about one-half of the United States' one million Indians now live in urban areas.

Identified are books and articles on what urbanization does to economic status; how it effects the Indian kinship system; the Indian assimilation—or lack thereof—into the urban American mainstream; as well as writings on the social problems which may accompany city life—alcohol, crime, and mental health problems.

There are 198 articles, books, and chapters in books listed on this topic. Of these, six are recommended as works for the beginner, and another fourteen are suggested for a basic library collection.

Subject heading: "Indians of North America—Urban residence."

*War*

Tebbel, John. *The Compact History of the Indian Wars.* New York: Hawthorn Books, 1966.

Going from east to west, and from 1607 to 1890, John Tebbel covers the wars between the Indians and the whites which took place in what is now the United States. Writing with the easy, narrative flow of the professional writer, Tebbel begins with the confrontation between Powhattan and Captain John Smith in 1607, describes King Philip's War in Massachusetts in 1675–76, and, with a once-over-lightly of all the wars in between, goes on to the Modoc War in Oregon in 1873, the fights with the Apaches in the Southwest in the 1880s, and ends with the bloodbath between the Sioux and the Seventh Cavalry at Wounded Knee, South Dakota in 1890.

This is a fast-paced popular history full of colorful anecdote. (At Pea Ridge, Arkansas, during the Civil War, Cherokee Chief John Ross rode into battle in his customary stove pipe hat and frock coat, sitting in an open carriage at the side of General Albert Pike who had donned Indian gear to emphasize to the Indians fighting on the Confederate side that the Confederates were their brothers. It did not do much good as the two Cherokee units on the Confederate side began to fight each other, and eventually Indians on both the North and South sides left for home, leaving the whites to fight it out between themselves. Later, after John Ross had defected to the North, taking most of the Cherokees with him, the Confederates captured the Cherokee capital of Tahlequah and burned Ross's home to the ground.)

There are no footnotes. There is a bibliography at the end for further reading.

Utley, Robert M., and Wilcomb E. Washburn. *The American Heritage History of the Indian Wars.* New York: American Heritage Publishing Co., 1977.

This is a large, slick-paper book of the coffee table type chock-full of pictures of the 300-year conflict between the Indians and the white.

The pictures range from contemporaneous black-and-white engravings and sketches made by soldiers or Indians on the spot to resplendent oil paintings completed long after the incidents they portray.

The subjects are scenes of torture, of capture of women and children (and of their later rescue), of fortifications, of skirmishes and full-fledged battles, of dying and dead heroes.

There are also pictures of the tools of war, of tomahawks and flintlocks, portraits of Indian warriors in full regalia or in the more somber garb of the white man, and portraits of the white warriors as well. There are photographs of army life in the garrison, of western scenery, of Indians gathered around trading posts, of missionaries, and more, including so much not directly related to fighting that this book could serve as supplementary reading for any study of this period in the history of Indian-white relations.

The artists include Benjamin West, George Catlin, Frederick Remington, and the photographer Edward S. Curtis.

The book is in two parts, the first focusing on the eastern United States and the second on the western United States. The amount of detail here in pictures and in words, the style of presentation, and the subject matter itself make this a book to be dipped into and consulted over a period of time rather than read through.

### Women

Katz, Jane B., ed. *I am the Fire of Time, the Voices of Native American Women*. New York: E. P. Dutton, 1977.

Snippets of autobiography from the standard anthropological works; interviews with contemporary women; poetry; and a few stories all on what it was—or is—like to be an American Indian woman.

Each entry has a short note from the editor giving background information, tribal history and beliefs, or biographical information on the interviewee.

Childbirth customs, growing up as an Indian girl, boarding school, early marriage, healing, widowhood, grinding poverty, modern-day reservation politics—are all discussed here in a few paragraphs or pages.

The book is illustrated with a few black and white photographs and drawings.

Niethammer, Carolyn. *Daughters of the Earth: the Lives and Legends of American Indian Women*. New York: Macmillan, 1977.

A little bit on a lot of tribes on what it was like to be an Indian girl and woman: to deliver your baby onto a patch of warm sand as a Hopi mother might; to have a four-day dance as a puberty celebration as an Apache girl could; to while away four days in a menstrual hut every month (so as not to pollute the men) as the Chickasaws and many others did; to be courted with flute music as a Crow girl might; to be married, at least for the first time, to a much older man, as a Gros Ventre girl might; to have your nose cut off for adultery as a Sioux woman might; to be a medicine woman and treat the sick as a Yurok, and the women of many other tribes did; to go to war with the men as an exceptional Cheyenne or Ojibwa woman might; to swim across the Missouri River with your child on your back as a Mandan woman could; to be raised as a boy if there were too many girls in the family as a Kaska might; and much more.

Customs, beliefs, and practices associated with birth, childhood, puberty, motherhood, widowhood, sexual practices in general – they are all described here.

The author's scope is all of North America, and she has taken the material on women out of context from the anthropological literature to put it all into one book; however, the bibliography is there citing the original sources for those who wish to read further, and it is all marvelously interesting.

Old-time Indian legends pertinent to the topic under discussion are sprinkled through the book, and there are a few black-and-white photographs of Indian women.

Subject heading: "Indians of North America – Women."

Part 3

*Unannotated
Bibliography
Alphabetically by Tribe*

This list gives the names of books on major tribes in the United States and Canada, excluding extinct tribes. It is arbitrarily limited to whole books on single tribes or closely affiliated tribal groups. It does not list dissertations, articles in journals, or books which cover many tribes or all of the tribes of a particular region. (These are the kinds of publications to check if information on the wanted tribe is not here.)

The tribal names were chosen primarily from two sources: *Linguistic and Cultural Affiliations of Canadian Indian Bands* (Ottawa: Department of Indian Affairs and Northern Development, 1967) and Theodore W. Taylor's *The States and Their Indian Citizens*, (Washington, D.C.: United States Department of the Interior, Bureau of Indian Affairs, 1972) which lists federally recognized tribes on pp. 238-245. (This same book also lists state reservations, Indian groups without trust land, and terminated tribes and groups — as of the 1960s. A more recent government publication listing "unacknowledged" tribes is "A Hearing before the Select Committee on Indian Affairs, United States Senate, Ninety-Sixth Congress, Second Session on Oversight of the Federal Acknowledgement Process and the Federal Acknowledgement Project of the Bureau of Indian Affairs, June 2, 1980.)"

I have preferred the more recent books most likely to be found in libraries. Older books, government publications, and titles from small, local publishers are listed only when they were the only ones I could identify.

Nearly all of the titles from two series are included. They are those of the Holt, Rinehart and Winston Case Studies in Cultural Anthropology, and the Indian Tribal Series published in Phoenix, Arizona.

The Case Studies in Cultural Anthropology are paperbacks designed for supplementary reading in anthropology classes. Written by teachers who have lived with the groups they write about, they are short, inexpensive, and widely available. They always have a good bibliography for further reading.

The books in the Indian Tribal Series are also short — about 100 pages. They were written in the 1970s and were "designed for readability [and] attempt to relate the past, describe the present, and predict something of the future of reservation populations with a minimum of technical jargon and without recourse to notes." Tribal officials reviewed each book before it was published. (Henry Dobyns, "Native American Publication of Cultural History," *Current Anthropology*, Vol. 15, No. 3, (September 1974), pp. 304-306.)

To compile this list I have benefited from Barbara Leitch's *Concise Dictionary of Indian Tribes of North America* (Algonac Mich.: Reference Publications, 1979); George Murdock and Timothy O'Leary's *Ethnographic Bibliographic of North America*, 4th ed. (New Haven: Human Relations Area Files Press, 1975); Francis Prucha's *A Bibliographical Guide to the History of Indian-white Relations in the United States* (Chicago: University of Chicago Press, 1977) and its 1975–1980 *Supplement* published by the University of Nebraska Press in 1982, and, most useful of all, the small books of the Newberry Library Center for the History of the American Indian Bibliographic Series which describe and recommend books for specific tribes or regions.

The spelling of tribal names at the head of each section follows that established by the Library of Congress (*Library of Congress Subject Headings*, v. 1, 1980, pp. 1130–1132), as this is the spelling to use in a library's card catalog to find more books on a particular tribe. A tribe's name in a book will frequently be spelled in a different way from that preferred by the Library of Congress (e.g., "Sarsi" is the spelling used by the Library of Congress, "Sarcee" is the spelling used in the book cited for that tribe).

Where the spelling is so different that alphabetic sequence is affected I have given a cross reference to the preferred spelling.

I have also provided cross references from popular names to those used by the Library of Congress (e.g., "Sioux" see "Dakota").

### Alabamu

Folsom-Dickerson, W. E. S. *The White Path*. San Antonio: The Naylor Co., 1965.

### Apache

Dobyns, Henry F. *The Apache People*. Phoenix: Indian Tribal Series, 1971.

Mails, Thomas E. *The People Called Apache*. Englewood Cliffs, N.J.: Prentice-Hall, 1974.

Worcester, Donald E. *The Apaches: Eagles of the Southwest*. Norman: University of Oklahoma Press, 1979.

See also: CIBECUE APACHE, JICARILLA APACHE, KIOWA (APACHE), MESCALERO APACHE, WESTERN APACHE.

### Arapaho

Trenholm, Virginia C. *The Arapahoes, Our People*. Norman: University of Oklahoma Press, 1970.

**Arikara** See **Three Affiliated Tribes**

**Assiniboin**

Writers' Program. Montana. *The Assiniboines: from the Accounts of the Old Ones Told to First Boy (James Larpenteur Long)*. Edited by Michael S. Kennedy. New ed. Norman: University of Oklahoma Press, 1961.

**Athapascan**

Van Stone, James W. *Athapaskan Adaptations; Hunters and Fishermen of the Subarctic Forests*. Chicago: Aldine, 1974.

**Atsina**

Flannery, Regina. *The Gros Ventres of Montana*. 2 vols. Washington, D.C.: Catholic University of America Press, 1953–1957.

**Bannock**

Madsen, Brigham D. *The Bannock of Idaho*. Caldwell, Idaho: The Caxton Printers, 1958.

**Beaver** See **Tsattine**

**Bellacoola**

Kopos, Cliff. *Bella Coola*. Vancouver: Mitchell Press, Ltd., 1970.
McIlwraith, Thomas F. *The Bella Coola Indians*. 2 vols. Toronto: University of Toronto Press, 1948.

**Blackfoot** See **Siksika**

**Brule**

Hyde, George E. *Spotted Tail's Folk*. Norman: University of Oklahoma Press, 1937.

**Cahuilla**

Bean, Lowell J. *Mukat's People: The Cahuilla Indians of Southern California*. Berkeley: University of California Press, 1973.

**Catawba**

Brown, Douglas S. *The Catawba Indians: The People of the River*. Columbia: University of South Carolina Press, 1966.
Hudson, Charles M. *The Catawba Nation*. Athens, GA.: University of Georgia Press, 1970.

## Cayuga

Wait, Mary Van Sickle, and William Heidt, Jr. *The Story of the Cayugas*. Ithaca, N.Y.: DeWitt Historical Society of Tompkins County, Inc., 1966.
See also **Iroquois**

## Cayuse

Ruby, Robert H., and John A. Brown. *The Cayuse Indians: Imperial Tribesmen of Old Oregon*. Norman: University of Oklahoma Press, 1972.

## Chemehuevi

Laird, Carobeth. *The Chemehuevi*. Banning, Calif.: Malki Museum Press, 1977.

## Cherokee

Gulick, John. *Cherokees at the Crossroads*. With an Epilogue by Sharlotte N. Williams. Rev. ed. Chapel Hill: Institute for Research in Social Science, University of North Carolina, 1973.
King, Duane H., ed. *The Cherokee Indian Nation: a Troubled History*. Knoxville: University of Tennessee Press, 1979.
Pierce, Earl Boyd, and Rennard Strickland. *The Cherokee People*. Phoenix: Indian Tribal Series, 1973.
Woodward, Grace S. *The Cherokees*. Norman: University of Oklahoma Press, 1963.

## Cheyenne

Berthong, Donald J. *The Southern Cheyennes*. Norman: University of Oklahoma Press, 1963.
Grinnell, George B. *The Cheyenne Indians: Their History and Ways of Life*. New Haven: Yale University Press, 1923. Reprint. Lincoln: University of Nebraska Press, 1972.
Hoebel, E. Adamson. *The Cheyennes: Indians of the Great Plains,* 2d ed. New York: Holt, Rinehart and Winston, 1978.
Marquis, Thomas B. *The Cheyennes of Montana*. Edited by Thomas D. Weiss. Algonac, Mich.: Reference Publications, 1978.

## Chickasaw

Baird, W. David. *The Chickasaw People*. Phoenix: Indian Tribal Series, 1974.
Gibson, Arrell M. *The Chickasaws*. Norman: University of Oklahoma Press, 1971.

**Chinook**

Ruby, Robert H., and John A. Brown. *The Chinook Indians: Traders of the Lower Columbia River*. Norman: University of Oklahoma Press, 1976.

**Chipewyan**

Van Stone, James W. *The Changing Culture of the Snowdrift Chipewyan*. Ottawa: National Museum of Canada, 1965.

**Chippewa**

Bishop, Charles A. *The Northern Ojibwa and the Fur Trade: an Historical and Ecological Study*. Toronto: Holt, Rinehart and Winston of Canada, 1974.

Danzinger, Edmund J. *The Chippewas of Lake Superior*. Norman: University of Oklahoma Press, 1979.

Dunning, Robert W. *Social and Economic Change Among the Northern Ojibwa*. Toronto: University of Toronto Press, 1959.

Landes, Ruth. *The Ojibwa Women*. New York: Norton, 1971.

Hickerson, Harold. *The Chippewa and Their Neighbors: a Study in Ethnohistory*. New York: Holt, Rinehart and Winston, 1970.

Paredes, J. Anthony, ed. *Anishinabe: 6 Studies of Modern Chippewa*. Tallahassee: University of Florida Press, 1980.

Roufs, Timothy. *The Anishinabe of the Minnesota Chippewa Tribe*. Phoenix: Indian Tribal Series, 1975.

**Chitimacha**

Hoover, Herbert. *The Chitimacha People*. Phoenix: Indian Tribal Series, 1975.

**Choctaw**

Baird, W. David. *The Choctaw People*. Phoenix: Indian Tribal Series, 1973.

Debo, Angie. *The Rise and Fall of the the Choctaw Republic*. 2d ed. Norman: University of Oklahoma Press, 1961.

De Rosier, Arthur H., Jr. *The Removal of the Choctaw Indians*. Knoxville: University of Tennessee Press, 1970. Reprint. New York: Harper and Row, 1972.

**Chumashan**

Landberg, Lief C. W. *The Chumash Indians of Southern California*. Los Angeles: Southwest Museum, 1965.

## Cibecue Apache

Basso, Keith. *The Cibecue Apache.* New York: Holt, Rinehart and Winston, 1970.

## Cochiti

Lange, Charles H. *Cochiti: a New Mexico Pueblo, Past and Present.* Austin: University of Texas Press, 1959.

## Cocopa

Williams, Anita Alvarez de. *The Cocopah People.* Phoenix: Indian Tribal Series, 1974.

## Colville

Gidley, Mick. *With One Sky Above Us: Life on an Indian Reservation at the Turn of a Century.* New York: G. P. Putnam's Sons, 1979.

## Comanche

Cash, Joseph, and Gerald Wolff. *The Comanche People.* Phoenix: Indian Tribal Series, 1974.

Wallace, Ernest, and E. Adamson Hoebel. *The Comanches: Lords of the South Plains.* Norman: University of Oklahoma Press, 1952.

## Conoy See Nanticoke

## Coushatta See Koasati

## Cree

Dusenberry, J. Verne. *The Montana Cree, a Study in Religious Persistence.* Stockholm: Almqvist and Wiksell, 1962.

Knight, Rolf. *Ecological Factors in Changing Economy and Social Organization Among the Rupert House Cree.* Ottawa: Queen's Printer and Controller of Stationery, 1968.

Mason, Leonard. *The Swampy Cree: A Study in Acculturation.* Ottawa: Queen's Printer, 1967.

Richardson, Boyce. *Strangers Devour the Land.* New York: Alfred A. Knopf, 1976.

## Creek

Debo, Angie. *The Road to Disappearance.* New ed. Norman: University of Oklahoma Press, 1976.

Green, Donald E. *The Creek People*. Phoenix: Indian Tribal Series, 1973.

## Crow

Lowie, Robert H. *The Crow Indians*. New York: Farrar and Rinehart, 1935.

McGinnis, Dale K., and Floyd W. Sharrock. *The Crow People*. Phoenix: Indian Tribal Series, 1972.

## Dakota

Hassrick, Royal B. *The Sioux: Life and Customs of a Warrior Society*. Norman: University of Oklahoma Press, 1964.

Lawson, Michael L. *Dammed Indians: the Pick-Sloan Plan and the Missouri River Indians*. Norman: University of Oklahoma Press, 1982.

Sandoz, Mari. *These Were the Sioux*. New York: Hastings House, 1961. Reprint. New York: Dell Publishing Co., 1967.

See also BRULE, MDEWKANTON, OGLALA, ROSEBUD, SANTEE

## Delaware

Weslager, Clinton A. *The Delaware Indians, a History*. New Brunswick: Rutgers University Press, 1972.

## Diegueno

Cuero, Delfina. *The Autobiography of Delfina Cuero, a Diegueno Indian*. As told to Florence C. Shipek. Interpreter: Rosalie Pinto Robertson. Banning, Calif.: Malki Museum Press, 1970.

## Dogrib See Thlingchadinne

## Flathead See Salish

## Fox

Gearing, Frederick O. *The Face of the Fox*. Chicago: Aldine Publishing Co., 1970.

See also **Sauk**

## Gros Ventre See Atsina

## Haida

Blackman, Margaret B. *During My Time, Florence Edenshaw*

*Davidson, a Haida Woman.* Seattle: University of Washington Press, 1982.

Stearns, Mary Lee. *Haida Culture in Custody.* Seattle: University of Washington Press, 1981.

Van den Brink, J. H. *The Haida Indians: Cultural Change Mainly Between 1876–1970.* Leiden: E. J. Brill, 1974.

## Han

Osgood, Cornelius. *The Han Indians: A Compilation of Ethnographic and Historical Data on the Alaska–Yukon Boundary Area.* New Haven: Yale University, Department of Anthropology, 1971.

## Hare See **Kawchottine**

## Havasupai

Dobyns, Henry, and Robert Euler. *The Havasupai People.* Phoenix: Indian Tribal Series, 1971.

Hirst, Stephen. *Life in a Narrow Place.* New York: David McKay Co., 1976.

## Hidatsa

Bowers, Alfred W. *Hidatsa Social and Ceremonial Organization.* Washington, D.C.: GPO, 1965.

See also **Three Affiliated Tribes**

## Hopi

Titiev, Mischa. *The Hopi Indians of Old Oraibi: Change and Continuity.* Ann Arbor: University of Michigan Press, 1972.

Thompson, Laura. *Culture in Crisis: A Study of the Hopi Indians.* New York: Harper, 1950. Reprint. New York: Russell and Russell, 1973.

Yava, Albert. *Big Falling Snow: A Tewa-Hopi Indian's Life and Times and the History and Traditions of His People.* Edited by Harold Courlander. New York: Crown Publishers, 1978.

## Hualapai

Dobyns, Henry F., and Robert Euler. *The Walapai People* Phoenix: Indian Tribal Series, 1976.

Dobyns, Henry F. *Wauba Yuma's People: the Comparative Socio-Political Structure of the Pai Indians of Arizona.* Prescott, Ariz: Prescott College Press, 1970.

## Iowa

Blaine, Martha R. *The Ioway Indians*. Norman: University of Oklahoma Press, 1979.

## Iroquois

Fenton, William N., ed. *Parker on the Iroquois*. Syracuse: Syracuse University Press, 1968.

Hauptman, Laurence M. *The Iroquois and the New Deal*. Syracuse: Syracuse University Press, 1981.

Tooker, Elizabeth. *The Iroquois Ceremony at Midwinter*. Syracuse: Syracuse University Press, 1970.

Wilson, Edmund. *Apologies to the Iroquois*. With a Study of the Mohawks in High Steel, by Joseph Mitchell. New York: Farrar, Straus and Cudahy, 1960.

See also CAYUGA, MOHAWK, ONEIDA, ONONDAGA, SENECA, TUSCARORA.

## Jicarilla Apache

Gunnerson, Dolores A. *The Jicarilla Apaches: a Study in Survival*. DeKalb: Northern Illinois University Press, 1974.

## Kalispel

Carriker, Robert. *The Kalispel People*. Phoenix: Indian Tribal Series, 1973.

## Kansa

Unrau, William E. *The Kansa Indians: a History of the Wind People, 1673-1873*. Norman: University of Oklahoma Press, 1971.

Unrau, William E. *The Kaw People*. Phoenix: Indian Tribal Series, 1975.

## Kaska

Honigmann, John J. *The Kaska Indians: an Ethnographic Reconstruction*. New Haven: Yale University, Department of Anthropology, 1954.

## Kaw See Kansa

## Kawchottine

Savishinsky, Joel S. *The Trail of the Hare: Life and Stress in an Arctic Community*. New York: Gordon and Breach, 1974.

## Kenaitze See Tanai

## Kickapoo

Gibson, Arrell M. *The Kickapoos: Lords of the Middle Border.* Norman: University of Oklahoma Press, 1963.

Nielsen, George. *The Kickapoo People.* Phoenix: Indian Tribal Series, 1975.

## Kiowa

Mayhall, Mildred P. *The Kiowas.* Norman: University of Oklahoma Press, 1962.

## Kiowa (Apache)

Whitewolf, Jim. *Jim Whitewolf: the Life of a Kiowa Apache.* Edited by Charles S. Brant. New York: Dover Publications, 1969.

## Klamath

Stern, Theodore. *The Klamath Tribe: a People and Their Reservation.* Seattle: University of Washington Press, 1965.

## Koasati

Johnson, Bobby. *The Coushatta People.* Phoenix: Indian Tribal Series, 1976.

## Kutchin

Nelson, Richard K. *Hunters of the Northern Forest: Designs for Survival Among the Alaskan Kutchin.* Chicago: University of Chicago Press, 1973.

## Kutenai

Turney-High, Harry H. *Ethnography of the Kutenai.* Menasha, Wis.: The American Anthropological Association, 1941.

## Kwakiutl

Goldman, Irving. *The Mouth of Heaven, an Introduction to Kwakiutl Religious Thought.* New York: John Wiley, 1975.

Rohner, Ronald P., and Evelyn C. Rohner. *The Kwakiutl: Indians of British Columbia.* New York: Holt, Rinehart and Winston, 1970.

Spradley, James P., ed. *Guests Never Leave Hungry: the Autobiography of James Sewid, a Kwakiutl Indian.* New Haven: Yale University Press. New ed. Montreal: McGill-Queen's University Press, 1972.

## Luiseno

Sparkman, Philip S. *The Culture of the Luiseno Indians*. Berkeley: California University Publication in American Archaeology and Ethnology 8, 1908. Reprint. Ramona, Calif.: Acoma Books, 1971.

## Lumbee

Blu, Karen I. *The Lumbee Problem: the Making of an American Indian People*. Cambridge, England: Cambridge University Press, 1980.

Dial, Adolph L., and David K. Eliades. *The Only Land I Know: A History of the Lumbee Indians*. San Francisco: Indian Historian Press, 1975.

## Lummi

Stern, Bernhard J. *The Lummi Indians of Northwest Washington*. New York: Columbia University Press, 1934.

## Makah

Colson, Elizabeth. *The Makah Indians: A Study of an Indian Tribe in Modern American Society*. Minneapolis: University of Minnesota Press, 1953. Reprint. Westport, Conn.: Greenwood Press, 1974.

## Malecite

Wallis, Wilson D., and Ruth Wallis. *The Malecite Indians of New Brunswick*. National Museum of Canada Bulletin 148. Ottawa, 1957.

## Mandan

Bowers, Alfred W. *Mandan Social and Ceremonial Organization*. Chicago: University of Chicago Press, 1950.
See also **Three Affiliated Tribes**

## Maricopa

Spier, Leslie. *Yuman Tribes of the Gila River*. Chicago: University of Chicago Press, 1933. Reprint. Totowa, N.J.: Cooper Square, 1970.

## Mdewakanton

Landes, Ruth. *The Mystic Lake Sioux*. Madison: University of Wisconsin Press, 1968.

## Menominee

Ourada, Patricia K. *The Menominee Indians: a History*. Norman: University of Oklahoma Press, 1979.

Peroff, Nicholas C. *Menominee Drums: Tribal Termination and Restoration, 1954–1974*. Norman: University of Oklahoma Press, 1982.

Spindler, George, and Louis Spindler. *Dreamers Without Power, the Menomini Indians*. New York: Holt, Rinehart and Winston, 1971.

## Mescalero Apache

Dobyns, Henry. *The Mescalero Apache People*. Phoenix: Indian Tribal Series, 1973.

Opler, Morris. *Apache Odyssey: A Journey Between Two Worlds*. New York: Holt, Rinehart and Winston, 1969.

Sonnichsen, Charles L. *The Mescalero Apaches*. 2d ed. Norman: University of Oklahoma Press, 1973.

## Metis

Redbird, Duke. *We Are Metis, A Metis View of the Development of a Native Canadian People*. Willowdale, Ontario: Ontario Metis and Non-Status Indian Association, 1980.

## Miami

Anson, Bert. *The Miami Indians*. Norman: University of Oklahoma Press, 1970.

## Micmac

Bock, Philip K. *The Micmac Indians of Restigouche: History and Contemporary Description*. Ottawa: Department of the Secretary of State, 1966.

Wallis, Wilson D., and Ruth S. Wallis. *The Micmac Indians of Eastern Canada*. Minneapolis: University of Minnesota, 1955.

## Mimbres Apache

Thrapp, Dan L. *Victorio and the Mimbres Apaches*. Norman: University of Oklahoma Press, 1974.

## Missouri See Oto-Missouri

## Miwok

Corrotto, Eugene L. *Miwok Means People*. Fresno, Calif.: Valley Publishers, 1973.

## Modoc

Faulk, Odie. *The Modoc People*. Phoenix: Indian Tribal Series, 1976.
Ray, Verne F. *Primitive Pragmatists: the Modoc Indians of Northern California*. Seattle: University of Washington Press, 1963.

## Mohave

Grey, Herman. *Tales From the Mohave*. With a foreword by Alice Marriott. Norman: University of Oklahoma Press, 1970.
Sherer, Lorraine M. *The Clan System of the Fort Mohave Indians*. Los Angeles: Historical Society of Southern California, 1965.

## Mohawk

Blanchard, David. *Seven Generations: A History of the Kanienke-haka*. Kanawake, Quebec: Center for Curriculum Development, Kanawake Survival School, 1980. [A social studies textbook.]
See also **Iroquois**

## Montagnais

Harper, Francis. *The Friendly Montagnais and Their Neighbors in the Ungava Peninsula*. Lawrence: University of Kansas, 1964.
McGee, John T. *Cultural Stability and Change Among the Montagnais Indians of the Lake Melville Region of Labrador*. Washington, D.C.: Catholic University of America Press, 1961.

## Moors See **Nanticoke**

## Nanticoke

Weslager, Clinton A. *Delaware's Forgotten Folk: the Story of the Moors and Nanticokes*. Philadelphia: University of Pennsylvania Press, 1943.
_____. *The Nanticoke Indians: a Refugee Tribal Group of Pennsylvania*. Harrisburg: Pennsylvania Historical and Museum Commission, 1948.

## Narraganset

Boissevain, Ethel. *The Narragansett People*. Phoenix: Indian Tribal Series, 1975.

## Nascapee

Henrikson, George. *Hunters in the Barrens: the Naskapi on the Edge of the White Man's World*. St. John's: Memorial University of Newfoundland, 1973.

Speck, Frank G. *Naskapi: the Savage Hunters of the Labrador Peninsula*. Norman: University of Oklahoma Press, 1935.

## Navaho

Kluckhohn, Clyde, and Dorothea C. Leighton. *The Navajo*. Rev. ed. by Lucy H. Wales and Richard Kluckhohn. Cambridge: Harvard University Press, 1974.

Underhill, Ruth. *The Navajos*. Rev. ed. Norman: University of Oklahoma Press, 1967.

Yazzie, Ethelou, ed. *Navajo History*. Chinle, Ariz.: Navajo Community College Press for the Navajo Curriculum Center, Rough Rock Demonstration School, 1971.

## Nespelim See Sanpoil

## Nez Perce

Haines, Francis. *The Nez Perces*. Norman: University of Oklahoma Press, 1955.

## Nisqualli

Smith, Marion W. *The Puyallup-Nisqually*. New York: Columbia University Press, 1940.

## Nootka

Drucker, Philip. *The Northern and Central Nootkan Tribes*. Washington, D.C.: GPO, 1951.

## Oglala

Hyde, George E. *Red Cloud's Folk*. Norman: University of Oklahoma Press, 1937.

Walker, James R. *Lakota Society*. Edited by Raymond DeMallie. Lincoln: University of Nebraska Press, 1982.

## Ojibwa See Chippewa

## Omaha

Fletcher, Alice C., and Francis LaFlesche. *The Omaha Tribe*. Washington, D.C.: GPO, 1905–1906.

Mead, Margaret. *The Changing Culture of an Indian Tribe*. New York: Columbia University Press, 1932. Reprint. New York: AMS, 1969.

## Oneida

Richards, Cara. *The Oneida People*. Phoenix: Indian Tribal Series, 1974.
See also **Iroquois**

## Onondaga

Clark, Joshua V. H. *Onondaga; or Reminiscences of Earlier and Later Times* . . . Syracuse, N.Y.: Stoddard and Babcock, 1849. Reprint. Millwood, N.Y.: Kraus Reprint, 1973.
See also **Iroquois**

## Osage

Baird, W. David. *The Osage People*. Phoenix: Indian Tribal Series, 1972.
Mathews, John J. *Wah'kon-tah: the Osage and the White Man's Road*. Norman: University of Oklahoma Press, 1932. Reprinted.
_____. *The Osages: Children of the Middle Waters*. Norman: University of Oklahoma Press, 1961. Reprint, 1973.

## Oto-Missouri

Chapman, Berlin B. *The Otoes and Missourias: a Study of Indian Removal and the Legal Aftermath*. Oklahoma City: Times Journal Publishing Co., 1965.
Edmunds, R. David. *The Otoe-Missouria People*. Phoenix: Indian Tribal Series, 1976.

## Ottawa

Cash, Joseph H., and Gerald W. Wolff. *The Ottawa People*. Phoenix: Indian Tribal Series, 1976.

## Paiute

Euler, Robert. *The Paiute People*. Phoenix: Indian Tribal Series, 1972.
Inter-Tribal Council of Nevada. *NUMA: A Northern Paiute History*. Reno: Inter-tribal Council of Nevada, 1976.
_____. *NUWUVI: A Southern Paiute History*. Reno: Intertribal Council of Nevada, 1976.
Johnson, Edward C. *Walker River Paiute: A Tribal History*. Schurz, Nevada: Walker River Paiute Tribe, 1975.

## Papago

Dobyns, Henry. *The Papago People*. Phoenix: Indian Tribal Series, 1972.

Joseph, Alice, Rosamond B. Spicer, and Jane Chesky. *The Desert People: A Study of the Papago Indians*. Chicago: University of Chicago Press, 1949.

### Pawnee

Hyde, George E. *Pawnee Indians*. Denver: University of Denver Press, 1951. Reprint. University of Oklahoma Press, 1973.
Tyson, Carl. *The Pawnee People*. Phoenix: Indian Tribal Series, 1976.
Weltfish, Gene. *The Lost Universe with a Closing Chapter on the Universe Regained*. New York: Basic Books, 1965.

### Penobscot

Speck, Frank G. *Penobscot Man: the Life History of a Forest Tribe in Maine*. Philadelphia: University of Pennsylvania Press, 1940.

### Pima

Webb, George. *A Pima Remembers*. Tucson: University of Arizona Press, 1959.

### Ponca

Cash, Joseph H. *The Ponca People*. Phoenix: Indian Tribal Series, 1975.
Howard, James H. *The Ponca Tribe*. Washington, D.C.: GPO, 1965.

### Potawatomi

Cash, Joseph H. *The Potawatomi People*. Phoenix: Indian Tribal Series, 1976.
Clifton, James A. *The Prairie People: Continuity and Change in Potawatomi Indian Culture, 1665-1965*. Lawrence: Regents Press of Kansas, 1977.
Edmunds, R. David. *The Potawatomis: Keepers of the Fire*. Norman: University of Oklahoma Press, 1978.

### Pueblo

Dozier, Edward P. *The Pueblo Indians of North America*. New York: Holt, Rinehart and Winston, 1970.
Erdoes, Richard. *The Rain Dance People, the Pueblo Indians, Their Past and Present*. New York: Alfred A. Knopf, 1976.
Sando, Joe S. *The Pueblo Indians*. San Francisco: Indian Historian Press, 1976.

### Puyallup See Nisqualli

## Quapaw

Baird, W. David. *The Quapaw People*. Phoenix: Indian Tribal Series, 1975.

Baird, W. David. *The Quapaw Indians: A History of the Downstream People*. Norman: University of Oklahoma Press, 1980.

## Quechan (Yuma)

Bee, Robert L. *Crosscurrents Along the Colorado: the Impact of Government Policy on the Quechan Indians*. Tucson: University of Arizona Press, 1981.

See also **Yuma**

## Quileute

Powell, Jay, and Vickie Jensen. *Quileute: an Introduction to the Indians of LaPush*. Seattle: University of Washington Press, 1976.

## Quinault

Olson, Ronald L. *The Quinault Indians and Adze, Canoe, and House Types of the Northwest Coast*. 1927 and 1936. Reprint. Seattle: University of Washington Press, 1967.

## Rosebud

Cash, Joseph H. *The Sioux People (Rosebud)*. Phoenix: Indian Tribal Series, 1971.

## Sac See **Sauk**

## Salish

Barnett, Homer G. *The Coast Salish of British Columbia*. Eugene: University of Oregon Press, 1955.

Fahey, John. *The Flathead Indians*. Norman: University of Oklahoma Press, 1971.

## Sanpoil and Nespelim

Ray, Verne F. *The Sanpoil and Nespelem, Salishan Peoples of Northeastern Washington*. Seattle: University of Washington Press, 1933. Reprint. New Haven: Human Relations Area Files, 1954.

## Santee

Meyer, Roy W. *History of the Santee Sioux*. Lincoln: University of Nebraska Press, 1967.

**Sarsi**

Jenness, Diamond. *The Sarcee Indians of Alberta.* Ottawa, [J. O. Patenaude, printer, 1938]. (Canada. National Museum of Canada. Bulletin no. 90. Anthropological series no. 23)

**Sauk**

Hagen, William T. *The Sac and Fox Indians.* Norman: University of Okalahoma Press, 1958.

**Sekani**

Jenness, Diamond. *The Sekani Indians of British Columbia.* Ottawa: J. O. Patenaude, printer, 1937. (Canada. Dept. of Mines and Resources. Bulletin no. 84. National Museum of Canada. Anthropological ser. no. 20)

**Seminole**

Fairbanks, Charles. *The Seminole People.* Phoenix: Indian Tribal Series, 1973.

Garbarino, Merwyn S. *Big Cypress, a Changing Seminole Community.* New York: Holt, Rinehart and Winston, 1972.

McReynolds, Edwin C. *The Seminoles.* Norman: University of Oklahoma Press, 1957.

**Seneca**

Abrams, George. *The Seneca People.* Phoenix: Indian Tribal Series, 1976.

Wallace, Anthony F. C. *The Death and Rebirth of the Seneca.* New York: Alfred A. Knopf, 1970.

See also **Iroquois**

**Shawnee**

Clark, Jerry E. *The Shawnees.* Lexington: University Press of Kentucky, 1977.

Howard, James H. *Shawnee! The Ceremonialism of a Native Indian Tribe and Its Cultural Background.* Athens, Ohio: Ohio University Press, 1981.

**Shoshoni**

Inter-Tribal Council of Nevada. *NEWE: A Western Shoshone History.* Reno: Inter-tribal Council of Nevada, 1976.

Trenholm, Virginia C., and Maurice Carley. *The Shoshonis, Sentinels of the Rockies*. Norman: University of Oklahoma Press, 1964.

### Siksika (Blackfeet)

Ewers, John C. *The Blackfeet: Raiders on the Northwestern Plains*. Norman: University of Oklahoma Press, 1958.

McFee, Malcolm. *Modern Blackfeet*. New York: Holt, Rinehart and Winston, 1972.

### Sioux See Dakota

### Skagit

Collins, June M. *Valley of the Spirits*. Seattle: University of Washington Press, 1974.

### Slave

Honigmann, John J*J thnography and Acculturation of the Fort Nelson Slave. Notes on the Indians of the Great Slave Lake Area*, by J. Alden Mason. New Haven: Yale University Press, 1946.

### Spokan

Ruby, Robert H., and John A. Brown. *The Spokane Indians, Children of the Sun*. Norman: University of Oklahoma Press, 1970.

### Tache See Yokuts

### Tahltan

Emmons, George T. The *Tahltan Indians*. Phildelphia: The University Museum, 1911. Reprint. Atlantic Highlands, N.J.: Humanities, 1979.

### Tanai

Ackerman, Robert E. *The Kenaitze People*. Phoenix: Indian Tribal Series, 1975.

### Thlingchadinne

Helm, June, and Nancy O. Lurie. *The Subsistence Economy of the Dogrib Indians of Lac La Marte*. Ottawa: Department of Northern Affairs and Natural Resources, 1961.

### Three Affiliated Tribes of Ft. Berthold

Cash, Joseph, and Gerald Wolff. *The Three Affiliated Tribes*. Phoenix: Indian Tribal Series, 1974.

Meyer, Roy W. *The Village Indians of the Upper Missouri: The Mandans, Hidatsas, and Arikaras*. Lincoln: University of Nebraska Press, 1977.
See also **Atsina, Hidatsa, Mandan**

## Tlingit

DeLaguna, Frederica. *Under Mount Saint Elias: The History and Culture of the Yokutat Tlingit*. Washington, D.C.: Smithsonian Institution Press, 1972.
Oberg, Kalvero. *The Social Economy of the Tlingit Indians*. Seattle: University of Washington Press, 1973.

## Tolowa

Drucker, Philip. *The Tolowa and Their Southwest Oregon Kin*. Berkeley: University of California Press, 1937.

## Tsattine

Brody, Hugh. *Maps and Dreams: Indians and the British Columbia Frontier*. London: J. Norman and Hobhouse, 1982.

## Tsimshian

Garfield, Viola E., and Paul S. Wright. *The Tsimshian Indians and Their Arts*. Seattle: University of Washington Press, 1966.

## Tuscarora

Graymont, Barbara, ed. *Fighting Tuscarora: The Autobiography of Chief Clinton Rickard*. Syracuse: Syracuse University Press, 1973.
Johnson, F. Roy. *The Tuscaroras*. 2 vols. Murfreesboro, N.C.: Johnson Publishing Co., 1967–1968.
Williams, Ted C. *The Reservation*. Syracuse: Syracuse University Press, 1976. [Stories based on Tuscarora reservation life.]
See also **Iroquois**

## Ute

Delaney, Robert *The Southern Ute People*. Phoenix: Indian Tribal Series, 1974.
Jefferson, James, Robert W. Delaney, and Gregory C. Thompson. *The Southern Utes: A Tribal History*. Ignacio, Colo.: The Southern Ute Tribe, 1972.
Smith, Anne M. *Ethnography of the Northern Utes*. Museum of New Mexico Papers in Anthropology 17. Sante Fe, 1974.

Uintah-Ourary Ute Tribe. *A Brief History of the Ute People*. Fort Duchesne, Utah: Uintah-Ourary Ute Tribe, 1977.

## Walapai See Hualapai

## Wampanoag

Travers, Milton A. *The Wampanoag Indian Federation of the Algonquin Nation; Indian Neighbors of the Pilgrims*. Boston: Christopher Publishing House, 1961.

## Warm Springs

Philips, Susan U. *The Invisible Culture: Communication in Classroom and Community on the Warm Springs Indian Reservation*. New York: Longman, 1982.

## Washo

Downs, James F. *The Two Worlds of the Washo, an Indian Tribe of California and Nevada*. New York: Holt, Rinehart and Winston, 1966.

Inter-Tribal Council of Nevada. *WA SHE SHU: A Washo Tribal History*. Reno: Intertribal Council of Nevada, 1976.

## Western Apache

Goodwin, Grenville. *The Social Organization of the Western Apache*. Chicago: University of Chicago Press, 1942.

## Wichita

Newcomb, William W. *The People Called Wichita*. Phoenix: Indian Tribal Series, 1976.

## Winnebago

Radin, Paul. *The Winnebago Tribe*. Washington, D.C.: GPO, 1915. Reprint. New York: Johnson Reprint Co. 1971.

## Yakima

Daugherty, Richard D. *The Yakima People*. Phoenix: Indian Tribal Series, 1973.

Guie, H. Dean. *Tribal Days of the Yakima*. Yakima, Wash. Republic Publishing Co., 1937.

## Yaqui

Kelley, Jane H. *Yaqui Women: Contemporary Life Histories*. Lincoln: University of Nebraska Press, 1978.

Moises, Rosalio. *A Yaqui Life: The Personal Chronicle of a Yaqui Indian.* Lincoln: University of Nebraska Press, 1977.

Spicer, Edward H. *The Yaquis: A Cultural History.* Tucson: University of Arizona Press, 1980.

## Yavapai

Gifford, Edward W. *Northeastern and Western Yavapai.* Berkeley: University of California Press, 1936.

_____. *The Southeastern Yavapai.* Berkeley: University of California Press, 1930. Millwood, N.Y.: Kraus Reprint, 1965.

## Yokuts

Cummins, Marjorie W. *The Tache-Yokuts, Indians of the San Joaquin Valley: Their Lives, Songs, and Stories.* 2d ed., rev. Fresno, Calif.: Pioneer Publishing Co., 1979.

Latta, Frank F. *Handbook of the Yokuts Indian.* Bakersfield, Calif.: Kern County Museum, 1949.

## Yuma

Forbes, Jack D. *Warriors of the Colorado.* Norman: University of Oklahoma Press, 1965.

See also **Quechan**

## Zuni

Crampton, C. Gregory. *The Zunis of Cibola.* Salt Lake City: University of Utah Press, 1977.

Zuni People. *The Zunis, Self-Portrayals.* Albuquerque: University of New Mexico Press, 1972.

# 6

# Notes

## Chapter 2. Indexes

1. *Readers' Guide to Periodical Literature*. New York: H.W. Wilson, 1900–.

2. *Alternative Press Index*. Baltimore, Md.: Alternative Press Center, 1969–.

3. *Canadian Periodical Index. Index de Periodiques Canadiens*. Ottawa: Canadian Library Association, 1948–.

4. *Social Sciences Index*. New York: H.W. Wilson, 1974–.

5. *Humanities Index*. New York: H.W. Wilson, 1974–.

6. *Social Sciences and Humanities Index*. New York: H.W. Wilson, 1965–1974.

7. *International Index*. New York: H.W. Wilson, 1907–1965.

8. *Education Index*. New York: H.W. Wilson, 1929–.

9. *Current Index to Journals in Education*. Phoenix, Ariz.: Oryx Press, 1969–.

10. *Art Index*. New York: H.W. Wilson, 1929–.

11. *Business Periodicals Index*. New York: H.W. Wilson, 1958–.

12. *Public Affairs Information Service Bulletin*. New York: Public Affairs Information Service, Inc., 1915–.

13. *Cumulative Subject Index to the Public Affairs Information Service Bulletins, 1915–1974*. 15 vols. Arlington, Va.: Carrollton Press, 1977.

14. *International Bibliography of Social and Cultural Anthropology/ Bibliographie d'Anthropologie Social et Culturelle*, London: Tavistock Publications, 1955–.

15. *Anthropological Index to Current Periodicals in the Museum of Mankind Library* (Incorporating the Former *Royal Anthropological Institute Library*). London: Royal Anthropological Institute, 1963–.

16. *Anthropological Literature, an Index to Periodical Articles and Essays*. Comp. by Tozzer Library, Peabody Museum of Archaeology and Ethnology, Harvard University. South Salem, N.Y.: Redgrave Publishing Co., 1979–.

17. *Bibliographie Linguistique/Linguistic Bibliography*. Utrecht, Belgium: Spectrum, 1949–.

18. *MLA International Bibliography*. New York: Modern Language Association of America, 1921–.

19. *Religion Index One: Periodicals*. Continuing *Index to Religious Periodical Literature* Chicago: American Theological Library Association, 1953–.

20. *Social Sciences Citation Index.* Philadelphia: Institute for Scientific Information, 1966–.

21. *Arts and Humanities Citation Index.* Philadelphia: Institute for Scientific Information, 1978–.

22. *Index to Literature on the American Indian.* San Francisco: Indian Historian Press, 1970–1974.

23. *American Indian Index.* River Grove, Ill.: Russell L. Knor and Joseph A. Huebner, 1953–1968.

24. Douglas, Frederic A., comp. *A Guide to Articles on the American Indians in Serial Publications, Part I.* Denver: Denver Art Museum, 1934.

25. United States Department of the Interior. *Biographical and Historical Index of American Indians and Persons Involved in Indian Affairs.* 8 vols. Boston: G.K. Hall, 1966.

26. United States Bureau of American Ethnology. *List of Publications of the Bureau of American Ethnology with Index to Authors and Titles.* Washington, D.C.: Smithsonian Institution Press, 1971.

27. Miller, Mamie T. *Author, Title, and Subject Checklist of Smithsonian Institution Publications Relating to Anthropology.* University of New Mexico Bulletin No. 405, Bibliograhical Series, v. 1 no. 23. Albuquerque, N.M.: University of New Mexico Press, 1946.

28. Smithsonian Institution. Annual report. (Indexes). *Author-Subject Index to Articles in Smithsonian Annual Reports, 1849–1961.* Compiled by Ruth M. Stemple and the Editorial and Publications Division, Smithsonian Institution, Smithsonian Institution Publications 4503. Washington, D.C.: Smithsonian Institution, 1963.

29. *New York Times Index.* New York: New York Times Co., 1907–. [The volumes for 1851 to 1906 are published by R.R. Bowker Co.]

30. *Writings on American History*, 1903–. (Publisher varies. Volume for 1979/80 published by Kraus International Publications, Millwood, N.Y. [Copyright held by American Historical Association.]

31. *Cumulated Index Medicus.* Bethesda, Md.: National Library of Medicine, 1879–.

32. *Index to Current Urban Documents.* Westport, Conn.: Greenwood Press, 1972–.

33. *Catalogue of Government of Canada Publications.* Canadian Government Publishing Centre, Supply and Services Canada, Hull, Quebec, Canada, 1953–.

34. *Monthly Catalog of United States Government Publications.* Washington, D.C. GPO, 1895–.

35. *Combined Retrospective Index Set to Journals in History 1838–1974.* 11 vols. Arlington, Va.: Carrollton Press, 1977.

36. F.W. Faxon Co. *Cumulated Magazine Subject Index 1907–1949.* 2 vols. Boston: G.K. Hall, 1964.

37. Harzfeld, Lois A. *Periodical Indexes in the Social Sciences and Humanities.* Metuchen, N.J.: Scarecrow Press, 1978.

## Chapter 3. Abstracts

1. *America: History and Life.* Santa Barbara, Calif.: ABC-Clio, 1964–.

2. Smith, Dwight L. *Indians of the United States and Canada, a Bibliography*. Santa Barbara, Calif.: ABC-Clio, 1974.

3. *Resources in Education*. Washington, D.C.: U.S. Department of Education, National Institute of Education, 1966–.

4. *Current Index to Journals in Education*. Phoenix, Ariz.: Oryx Press, 1969–.

5. *Psychological Abstracts*. Washington, D.C.: American Psychological Association, 1927–.

6. *GeoAbstracts*. Norwich, England: Geo Abstracts, 1966–.

7. *Social Work Research and Abstracts*. New York: National Association of Social Workers, 1966–. [Continues *Abstracts for Social Workers*]

8. *Language and Language Behavior Abstracts*. San Diego, Calif.: Sociological Abstracts, 1967–.

9. *Women Studies Abstracts*. Rush, N.Y.: Rush Publishing Co., 1972–.

10. *Abstracts in Anthropology*. Farmingdale, N.Y.: Baywood Pub. Co., 1970–.

11. *Sociological Abstracts*. San Diego, Calif.: 1953–.

## Chapter 5. Library Catalogs

1. *Dictionary Catalog of the Department Library, United States Department of the Interior*. 37 vols. Washington, D.C. Boston: G.K. Hall, 1967.
_____. First Supplement. 4 vols. 1968.
_____. Second Supplement. 2 vols. 1971.
_____. Third Supplement. 4 vols. 1973.
_____. Fourth Supplement. 8 vols. 1975.

2. *Dictionary Catalog of the Edward E. Ayer Collection of Americana and American Indians*. 16 vols. The Newberry Library (Chicago). Boston: G.K. Hall, 1961.
_____. First Supplement. 3 vols. 1970.
_____. Second Supplement. 4 vols. 1980.

3. *Dictionary Catalog of the American Indian Collection in the Huntington Free Library and Reading Room*. 4 vols. (Bronx, New York). Boston: G.K. Hall, 1977.

4. *Catalogue of the Tozzer Library of the Peabody Museum of Archaeology and Ethnology, Harvard University*. 54 vols. (Former title: *Author and Subject Catalogues of the Library of the Peabody Museum of Archaeology and Ethnology, Harvard University*). Boston: G.K. Hall, 1963.
_____. First Supplement. 12 vols. 1970.
_____. Second Supplement. 6 vols. 1971.
_____. Third Supplement. 7 vols. 1975.
_____. Fourth Supplement. 7 vols. 1979.

5. *Tozzer Library Index to Anthropological Subject Headings*. 2d rev. ed. Boston: G.K. Hall, 1981.

6. Cleveland Public Library, John G. White Department. *Catalog of Folklore, Folklife and Folk Songs*. 3 vols. 2d ed. Boston: G.K. Hall, 1978.

7. New York Public Library. Research Libraries. *Dictionary Catalog of the History of the Americas Collection*. 28 vols. Boston: G.K. Hall, 1961.
_____. First Supplement. 9 vols. 1974.

8. American Philosophical Society, Philadelphia. Library. *Catalog of the Books in the American Philosophical Society Library.* 28 vols. Westport, Conn.: Greenwood Press, 1970.

9. Wisconsin. State Historical Society. Library. *Subject Catalog of the Library of the State Historical Society of Wisconsin, Madison, Wisconsin, Including the Pamphlet Subject Catalog Beginning in Volume 22.* 23 vols. Westport, Conn.: Greenwood Press, 1971.

10. American Antiquarian Society. Worcester, Mass. Library. *A Dictionary Catalog of American Books Pertaining to the 17th through 19th Centuries.* 20 vols. Westport, Conn.: Greenwood Press, 1971.

11. *Subject Catalog–Library of Congress*, Washington, D.C.: 1950–. [Published quarterly with annual and quinquennial cumulations.]

## Chapter 6. Handbooks, Encyclopedias, Dictionary

1. Hodge, Frederick Webb, ed. *Handbook of American Indians North of Mexico.* 2 vols. Bureau of American Ethnology Bulletin no. 30. Washington, D.C.: GPO, 1907–1910.

2. *Handbook of Indians of Canada.* Published as an Appendix to the Tenth Report of the Geographic Board of Canada. Ottawa, Printed by C.H. Parmelee, 1913. New York: Kraus Reprint, 1969.

3. Swanton, John R. *The Indian Tribes of North America*, Bureau of American Ethnology Bulleting 145. Washington, D.C.: GPO, 1952.

4. Sturtevant, William C., ed. *Handbook of North American* Indians. Washington, D.C.: Smithsonian Institution, 1978–.

5. Helm, June, ed. *Handbook of North American Indians.* Vol. 6, *Subarctic.* Washington, D.C.: Smithsonian Institution, 1981.

6. Heizer, Robert F. *Handbook of North American Indians.* Vol. 8, *California.* Washington, D.C.: Smithsonian Institution, 1978.

7. Ortiz, Alfonso, ed. *Handbook of North American Indians.* Vol. 9, *Southwest.* Washington, D.C.: Smithsonian Institution, 1979.

8. Trigger, Bruce G., ed. *Handbook of North American Indians.* Vol.15, *Indians of the Northeast.* Washington, D.C.: Smithsonian Institution, 1978.

9. Irvine, Keith, ed. *Encyclopedia of Indians of the Americas.* St. Clair Shores, Mich.: Scholarly Press, 1974–.

10. Spicer, Edward H. "American Indians." In *Harvard Encyclopedia of American Ethnic Groups.* Pp. 58–122. Cambridge, Mass.: The Belknap Press of Harvard University Press, 1980.

11. Leitch, Barbara A. *A Concise Dictionary of Indian Tribes of North America.* Algonac, Mich.: Reference Publications, 1979.

## Chapter 7. Directories, Catalogs, and Dissertation Sources

1. Gridley, Marion E., ed. *Indians of Today.* [n.p.] I.C.F.P. 1971.

2. Klein, Barry, ed. *Reference Encyclopedia of the American Indian.* 3d ed. 2 vols. Rye, N.Y.: Todd Publications, 1978.

3. *Native American Directory, Alaska, Canada, United States.* San Carlos, Ariz.: National Native American Co-operative, 1982.

4. *American Indian Reference Book.* Portage, Mich.: eARTh, 1976.

5. *Subject Guide to Books in Print.* New York: R.R. Bowker Co., 1957–.

6. *Canadian Books in Print, Subject Guide*. Toronto: University of Toronto Press, 1973–.

7. Danky, James P., ed. *Native American Periodicals and Newspapers, 1828–1982*. Westport, Conn.: Greenwood Press, 1983.

8. Katz, Bill, and Linda Sternberg Katz. *Magazines for Libraries*, 4th ed. New York: R.R. Bowker Co., 1982.

9. Weatherford, Elizabeth, *Native Americans on Film and Video*. New York: Museum of the American Indian, 1982.

10. U.S. Department of Commerce. *Federal and State Indian Reservations and Indian Trust Areas*. Rev. ed. Washington, D.C.: GPO, 1974.

11. Canada. Department of Indian Affairs and Northern Development. *Schedule of Indian Reserves and Settlements of Canada*. Ottawa, 1972.

12. Brascoupe, Simon, ed. *Directory of North American Indian Museums and Cultural Centers 1981*. Niagara Falls, N.Y.: North American Indian Museums Association, 1980.

13. *A Directory of Hispanic and American Indian Higher Education Programs*. Manuel J. Justiz . . . [et al.] with the research assistance of Virginia C. Higbie and compilation assistance of Annie S. David. Albuquerque, N.M. College of Education, University of New Mexico, 1980.

14. *College Blue Book*. 18th ed. 5 vols. New York: Macmillan, 1981.

15. Dockstader, Frederick J., comp. *The American Indian in Graduate Studies: A Bibliography of Theses and Dissertations*. 2d ed. Contributions from the Museum of the American Indian Heye Foundation. Vol. 25, pt. 1. New York: Museum of the American Indian, 1973.

———. 1974. *Supplement*. Contributions from the Museum of the American Indian. Vol. 25, pt. 2.

16. Nickerson, Gifford S. *Native North Americans in Doctoral Dissertations: a Classified and Indexed Research Bibliography*. Monticello, Ill.: Council of Planning Librarians, 1977. Council of Planning Librarians Exchange Bibliography #1232.

17. *Comprehensive Dissertation Index*, 1861–1972. 37 vols. Ann Arbor: Xerox University Microfilms. [Quinquennial and annual supplements to date.]

**Chapter 8. Archives and Government Documents**

1. U.S. Library of Congress. *National Union Catalog of Manuscript Collections*. 1959– (Imprint varies) [Updated regularly, usually once a year.]

2. *Union List of Manuscripts in Canadian Repositories–Catalogue Collectif des Manuscrits des Archives Canadiennes* Rev. ed. 2 vols. Ottawa: Public Archives of Canada, 1975.

———. *Supplement*. 1976.

———. *Supplement*. 1977–1978.

3. Hill, Edward E. *Guide to Records in the National Archives of the United States Relating to American Indians*. Washington, D.C., National Archives and Records Service, General Services Administration, 1981.

4. Ryan, Carmelita S. "The Written Record and the American Indian: Archives of the United States." *Western Historical Quarterly* 6, no. 2 (April 1975):163–173.

5. Smith, Jane S., and Robert M. Kvasnicka, eds. *Indian-White Relations, a Persistent Paradox*. Washington, D.C.: Howard University Press, 1981, pp. 13–32.

6. Public Archives Canada. Archives Publiques Canada. Public Records Division. *General Inventory Series. No. 1. Records Relating to Indian Affairs. (RG10)*. Compiled by Peter Gillis, David Hume and Robert Armstrong. Ottawa: 1975. [French and English]

7. Tate, Michael L. "Studying the American Indian Through Government Documents and the National Archives." *Government Publications Review, an International Journal* 5 (1978):285–294.

8. _____. "Red Power: Government Publications and the Rising Indian Activism of the 1970's." *Government Publications Review, an International Journal* 8A (1981): 499–518.

# Index*

---

*Tribal names are listed alphabetically in Part 3. They are not repeated in this index unless they are also book titles, in which case they are italicized.

*Books on American Indians and Eskimos*, 104
Bowden, Henry Warner, 107
Bowers, Alfred W., 130, 133
Bows and arrows, books on, 74–76
Brennan, Louis A., 68
*Brief History of the Ute People*, 143
Brody, Hugh, 142
Brown, Douglas S., 125
Brown, John A., 126, 127, 141
Brown, Marjorie J., 31
Brumble, H. David, 72
Bureau of American Ethnology, index to publications, 22
*Business Periodicals Index*, 17

CIS (*Congressional Information Service*), on-line data base, 34
Calender of events, 50
Call numbers, 5–8
Call numbers, Library of Congress, Indian-related, 8–11
Campbell, Lyle, 96
Canada, books on, 76–79
Canada, journals, 79
Canada, handbook on, 45
*Canadian Books in Print, Subject Index*, 51
*Canadian Indian Bibliography 1960–1970*, 77
*Canadian Indian Policy, a Critical Bibliography*, 78
*Canadian Journal of Native Education*, 88
Canadian material, indexed in, 41. *See also* Canadian studies
*Canadian Periodical Index. Index de Periodiques Canadiens*, 13n
Canadian studies, abstracted in, 25
Canadian studies, indexed in, 17
Captivities, indexed in, 42
Captivities, books on, 79–80
Card catalog, defined, 3
Card catalog, subject, 4
Carley, Maurice, 141
Carriker, Robert, 131
Case Studies in Cultural Anthropology, 123
*Cases and Materials on Federal Indian Law*, 99
Cash, Joseph, 128, 137, 138, 139, 141
Catalog cards, illustrations of, 6–7

*Catalog of Folklore, Folklife and Folk Songs*, 43–44
*Catalog of the Books in the American Philosophical Society Library*, 44
"Cataloging in Publication", 5
*Catalogue of Government of Canada Publications*, 23
*Catalogue of the Tozzer Library of the Peabody Museum . . . Harvard*, 43
*Catawba Indians: The People of the River*, 125
*Catawba Nation*, 125
*Cayuse Indians: Imperial Tribesmen of Old Oregon*, 126
Centres, education and friendship (Canada), 50
*Changing Culture of an Indian Tribe*, 136
*Changing Culture of the Snowdrift Chipewyan*, 127
Chapman, Berlin B., 137
*Chemehuevi*, 126
*Cherokee Indian Nation: a Troubled History*, 126
*Cherokee People*, 126
*Cherokees*, 126
*Cherokees at the Crossroads*, 126
Chesky, Jane, 138
*Cheyenne Indians: Their History and Ways of Life*, 126
*Cheyennes: Indians of the Great Plains*, 126
*Cheyennes of Montana*, 126
*Chickasaw People*, 126
*Chickasaws*, 126
*Child Abuse and Neglect*, on-line data base, 33–34
Child custody, abstracted in, 27
*Chinook Indians: Traders of the Lower Columbia River*, 127
*Chippewa and Their Neighbors*, 127
*Chippewas of Lake Superior*, 127
*Chitimacha People*, 127
*Choctaw People*, 127
*Chumash Indians of Southern California*, 127
*Cibecue Apache*, 128
Citation index, purpose of, 19
City documents, indexed in, 23
*Clan System of the Fort Mohave Indians*, 135
Clark, Jeffrey, 98
Clark, Jerry E., 140